Leader and Party
in Latin America

Westview Special Studies

The concept of Westview Special Studies is a response to the continuing crisis in academic and informational publishing. Library budgets for books have been severely curtailed. Ever larger portions of general library budgets are being diverted from the purchase of books and used for data banks, computers, micromedia, and other methods of information retrieval. Interlibrary loan structures further reduce the edition sizes required to satisfy the needs of the scholarly community. Economic pressures on the university presses and the few private scholarly publishing companies have severely limited the capacity of the industry to properly serve the academic and research communities. As a result, many manuscripts dealing with important subjects, often representing the highest level of scholarship, are no longer economically viable publishing projects--or, if accepted for publication, are typically subject to lead times ranging from one to three years.

Westview Special Studies are our practical solution to the problem. We accept a manuscript in camera-ready form, typed according to our specifications, and move it immediately into the production process. As always, the selection criteria include the importance of the subject, the work's contribution to scholarship, and its insight, originality of thought, and excellence of exposition. The responsibility for editing and proofreading lies with the author or sponsoring institution. We prepare chapter headings and display pages, file for copyright, and obtain Library of Congress Cataloging in Publication Data. A detailed manual contains simple instructions for preparing the final typescript, and our editorial staff is always available to answer questions.

The end result is a book printed on acid-free paper and bound in sturdy library-quality soft covers. We manufacture these books ourselves using equipment that does not require a lengthy make-ready process and that allows us to publish first editions of 300 to 1000 copies and to reprint even smaller quantities as needed. Thus, we can produce Special Studies quickly and can keep even very specialized books in print as long as there is a demand for them.

About the Book and Author

Tracing the development and decay of political parties in Latin America, Dr. Duff suggests that the sociological or environmental explanations of political parties are inadequate in explaining why institutionalized political parties develop in some societies and not in others. In a series of eight case studies of disparate Latin American nations in the 1920s and 1930s, Dr. Duff shows that the crucial factor in party institutionalism appears to be the emergence of political leaders who must rely on manipulation of institutions they create, rather than on personal charisma, for ultimate control of the political process. The successful institution builders--Calles in Mexico, Trujillo in the Dominican Republic, and Betancourt in Venezuela--are contrasted with notable failures--Yrigoyen in Argentina, Arturo Alessandri in Chile, Grau San Martín in Cuba, General Martinez in El Salvador, and Haya de la Torre in Peru.

Ernest A. Duff is chairman of the Department of Politics at Randolph-Macon Woman's College in Lynchburg, Virginia. He is the author of *Agrarian Reform in Colombia* and coauthor (with John F. McCamant) of *Violence and Repression in Latin America*.

Leader and Party
in Latin America

Ernest A. Duff

Westview Press / Boulder and London

This book is dedicated to the memory of
C. Alan Hutchinson.

Westview Special Studies on Latin America and the Caribbean

Published in 1985 in the United States of America by Westview Press, Inc.,
5500 Central Avenue, Boulder, Colorado 80301; Frederick A. Praeger,
Publisher

Library of Congress Cataloging in Publication Data
Duff, Ernest A.
    Leader and party in Latin America.
    (A Westview special study on Latin America and the Caribbean)
    Bibliography: p.
    Includes index.
    1. Political parties--Latin America. 2. Political
leadership--Latin America. I. Title.
JL969.A45D84 1985   324.2'2'098   84-25711
ISBN 0-8133-7019-1

Composition for this book was provided by the author
Printed and bound in the United States of America

10 9 8 7 6 5 4 3 2 1

Contents

Acknowledgments

The author accepts full responsibility for the content of this book, but nevertheless wishes to recognize the important contributions made by others.

Three of my colleagues, Susan Lockhart, Charlotte Stern, and Philip Thayer, read all or part of the manuscript. I am sure that their suggestions have vastly improved the final product.

My wife, Barbara, served as both editor and typist, especially in the early stages of this work. Ruth Bryan did the word processing on the final draft and helped me meet my deadlines.

Ernest A. Duff

Part 1
Introduction

Our images of Latin America in the 1920s and 1930s are vague and contradictory. On the one hand there is the caudillo, that comic-opera bemedalled general immortalized in H. L. Mencken's famous essay, "Gore in the Caribee." The other image is of inept and perhaps venal politicians, being seduced by rapacious Northamerican bankers, as presented in J. Fred Rippy's The Capitalists and Colombia. Yet, the two decades preceding World War II were of immense importance to an adequate understanding of Latin America of today; for it was during this period that political institutions were either created or destroyed, with the resultant political stability or chaos we observe today.

This is a study of the political leaders who produced those different types of political institutions, and how these institutions either have worked for or against the development of cohesive societies. Futher, it is a study of the relationship between the largely unexplored variable of political leadership and the environmental variables which have received most of the attention in writings on political parties' origins and development. More specifically, this study is an inquiry into the relation between political leadership and the development of modern political parties, and of the effect these parties have had upon the political life of various nations. Latin America is the locale for this book primarily because it presents such divergent cases of political leadership and subsequent political history. A major theme of this book is that certain political leaders in certain countries created and/or developed political parties capable of at least partially resolving the subsequent political crises through which these nations have passed, with a minimum of governmental repression or anti-systemic violence. Implicit in this theme is the idea that political development is not something that results from short-run forces within or without the polity; rather, the development of a cohesive society is a process that

1

takes decades. Current politics in Latin America are largely the result of events which occurred in those countries during the 1920s and 1930s, rather than in the 1970s and 1980s. The crucial factor determining whether or not these societies meet their current endogenous and exogenous challenges appears to be the development of strong political parties. These parties, where they exist, are able to satisfy in some measure the increased demand for participation in the political process by ever-increasing numbers of people. For it is a simple, stark fact that most Latin American nations have experienced vertiginous social mobilization since World War II, and the increased demands by citizens on their governments have placed incredible strains on their political systems. Only those nations which began developing strong, broad-based political parties during an earlier era appear to have met these demands without either a great deal of repression of dissident forces, or a great amount of violence, or both.[1]

A particularly crucial element in the development of Latin American political parties during the 1920s and 1930s appears to have been the political leadership exerted in each country during those decades. This was particularly true in Latin America, as this was the period of the caudillo, or strong man. Dictators with personalities many times larger than life dominated the scene in many countries. Even in countries where no real caudillo emerged, politics was conducted largely on a personal basis.[2] The caudillos are legendary: Gomez in Venezuela, Vargas in Brazil, Trujillo in the Dominican Republic, and Somoza in Nicaragua. The political bosses were there too: Calles in Mexico, Yrigoyen in Argentina, Alessandri in Argentina, and Batlle y Ordoñez in Uruguay all controlled the politics of these countries to an extraordinary degree. Opposition leaders, such as Betancourt and Caldera in Venezuela, Grau San Martin in Cuba, and Haya de la Torre in Peru, also participated in the politics of the time. The important point is not the locus of these leaders, but rather the influence each had on the development or decay of political parties during this period. Also crucial, of course, is the effect that the times themselves had on both the personalities who played roles in the political history of the period, and on the institutions that developed out of it. There is, of course, an interaction between the leader and the socal forces that surround him, and the influence of personality and leadership on the course of history varies from event to event.[3] Put simply, both social forces and leadership must be investigated in order to determine why, in some Latin American countries, modern broad-based political parties capable of resolving political crises have emerged; while in other Latin American countries these parties either do not exist or are so weak as to be ineffectual.[4]

To date, there are no studies dealing with the role of political leadership in the origin and development of political parties. There are, however, a number of studies of leadership in general, and political leadership in particular, which will serve as guides for this book.[5] Books and articles dealing with political parties are more numerous as political scientists have long recognized the crucial role that these institutions play in the political process.[6] However, none of the works on political parties deals with the element of political leadership in the genesis and development of these parties, and almost none of the works on political leadership relate that variable to the history of political institutions. Yet, as first glance, the type of leader who happens on the scene at a critical moment in the history of a political party appears to be a crucial element in political development or political decay as the modernization process moves inexorably forward.[7]

We propose, then, to utilize existing theories of leadership and political party development in order to examine the relation between leadership and party development in Latin America during the 1920s and 1930s. Further, we will examine the lives of several of these leaders in an effort to ascertain the types of political personality associated with both success and failure in developing long-lasting political institutions. It has already been demonstrated that the existence of strong political parties inhibits repression and violence in Latin America.[8] This should complete the causal chain: political leaders in the 1920s and 1930s, working within societal conditions that were, in most instances, favorable for political party development, either rose to the challenge of party development or failed in the attempt. These successes and failures were due in large part to the political personality of the leaders, as they meshed with the environmental conditions of particular societies. Where strong political parties were established, they have at least partially inhibited repression and violence in Latin America in recent years. Thus, the political leaders who held sway in the countries of Latin America fifty years ago have exerted a profound influence on the type of society--violent and repressive, or free and peaceful--in the Latin American countries today.

4

Notes

1. The importance of political parties in the political process has been noted by a number of writers. For an empirical assessment of their role in producing relative political peace in Latin America, see Ernest Duff and John McCamant, Violence and Repression in Latin America (New York: The Free Press, 1976), pp. 103-108.

2. See William A. Welsh, "Methodological Problems in the Study of Political Leadership in Latin America," Latin American Research Review, XI (Fall, 1978).

3. For an early statement of the problem of the interplay of individuals and events, see Sidney Hook, The Hero In History (New York: John Day, 1943). For a more sophisticated approach to the problem, see Fred Greenstein, "The Impact of Personality on Politics; An Attempt to Clear Away the Underbrush," American Political Science Review, 61 (1967), 629-641.

4. Ronald H. McDonald, Party Systems and Elections in Latin America (Chicago: Markham Publishing Company, 1971) and Jose Francisco Ruiz Massieu, Normacion Constitucional de los Partidos Politicos en America Latina (Mexico: Instituto de Investigaciones Juridicas, 1974) both provide comprehensive reviews of the political party situation in the nations of Latin America. The concept of the institutionalized political party is explained by Samuel P. Huntington, Political Order in Changing Societies (New Haven, Yale University Press, 1968), p. 12.

5. James MacGregor Burns' masterpiece, Leadership (New York: Harper and Row, 1978) must now be considered as the most important single source of knowledge concerning political leadership. Other works which have influenced this work are: Harold Lasswell, Psychopathology and Politics (Chicago, University of Chicago Press, 1931); Fred Greenstein, Personality and Politics (New York: W. W. Norton, 1969); Robert C. Tucker, Politics as Leadership (Columbia, Missouri: University of Missouri Press, 1981) Sidney Verba, Small Groups and Political Behavior (Princeton: Princeton University Press, 1961), Dankwart Rustow, Philosophers and Kings (New York: Braziller, 1970); James David Barber, The Presidential Character: Predicting Presidential Performance (Englewood Cliffs: Prentice Hall, 1977). In addition, several books by Erik Erikson, especially Young Man Luther and Identity: Youth and Crisis, have provided useful insights into the formation of leadership personality.

6. The most significant (in terms of this study) works on political parties are: Richard Hofstadter, The Idea of a Party System (Berkeley, California: University of California Press, 1969); Joseph LaPalombara and Myron Weiner, Political Parties and Political Development (Princeton, New Jersey, Princeton University Press,

1966); Maurice Duverger, _Political Parties_ (New York: John Wiley and Sons, 1963); Sigmund Neumann (ed.) _Modern Political Parties_ (Chicago: University of Chicago Press, 1956); and Avery Leiserson, _Parties and Politics_ (New York: Alfred A. Knopf, 1958). Additional works on political parties, which were of less importance to this study, are listed in the bibliography.

7. A number of authors have dealt with the phenomena of political development and political decay in the modernization process. Huntington's work, previously cited, is seminal.

8. Duff and McCamant, 115.

1
Political Leadership
and Political Parties

Latin American Political Leadership in the 1920s and 1930s

By the time Tad Szulc wrote Twilight of the Tyrants in the late 1950s most of the caudillos who had held sway over the nations of Latin America had either disappeared or were on the verge of being replaced by other, newer forms of government. Although Szulc's optimism over the explosion of democracy in Latin America proved unwarranted, the personalist dictatorship was largely a thing of the past.[1] Historical forces had made the caudillo, like the mastodon, obsolete. The 1920s and the 1930s were, on the other hand, the period of fullest flowering of the caudillo in Latin America. This was true in part because at that time Latin American countries (even the largest of them) could still be governed by one man. Societies had not yet become so complex that one person could not comprehend the basic political, economic, and social forces at work in one country. A dedicated bureaucrat like Trujillo in the Dominican Republic knew what was going on in "his" country. Admittedly, he needed the assistance of a secret police, plus a few informers, to ferret out opposition and to keep contending factions in line. Nevertheless, compared to the military regimes in Brazil, Chile, and other Latin American countries today, Trujillo's government was a one-man show.[2] Most Latin American countries during this period were characterized by low social mobilizaton, which meant that even in the larger nations of Latin America political leaders did not have to deal with an inordinate number of demands emanating from newly mobilized groups. As long as the caudillo could keep certain well-identified groups either happy or repressed, he could be reasonably sure that he would continue in power. Further, most of the problems with which the caudillo dealt were both non-technical and non-developmental. This meant that any shrewd, scheming boy could grow up to be dictator in any number of Latin American countries. Although Trujillo was the archetypical caudillo, he had his imitators and counterparts in other Latin American countries. Isidro Ayora in Ecuador, Jorge Ubico in Guatemala, Gerardo Machado and Fulgencio Batista in Cuba, Juan Vicente Gomez in Venezuela, and Rafael Franco in Paraguay were all worthy contenders for the title of caudillo.

At the same time, however, forces were at work which led to the appearance of a new type of caudillo dictator in some Latin American countries. Leaders of this second type "often rode to power on programs which seemed to offer panaceas for the social and economic ills of their nations."[3] The difference between the "new" and the "old" caudillos was largely one of style. The tactics of the new caudillos were openly mobilizational, in that they tried to enlist the active support of the growing middle class for their rule, while attempting to discredit and often humiliate the older ruling elite. The tacit political compact between the old elite and traditional caudillo was now discarded, and in its place arose a new symbiotic relationship between the "new" caudillo and the mass. I stated that the difference was largely one of tactics. The new caudillos were looking for a new power base for their rule, but their rule was still dictatorial and capricious in the style of the "old" caudillo. Getulio Vargas in Brazil, the prototype of the "new" caudillo propagandized more than did his old-style contemporaries, but the resulting political control and capricious one-man rule did not differ much from, say, Trujillo's government in the Dominican Republic; and the totality of control by one man over an entire nation was just as complete in Brazil as it was under Gomez in Venezuela.

The "new" caudillo was largely a product of historical forces at work in Latin America after World War I. The War had forced Latin American nations to industrialize at a much more rapid rate than previously. The Allied powers, with whom the Latin Americans had always exchanged their primary products for manufactured goods, suddenly were cut off as suppliers, as their industrial effort went for military hardware. The Latin American nations found it necessary to produce manufactured goods themselves, and this nascent industrialization inevitably resulted in the formation of a small but rapidly growing and politically conscious urban proletariat.

During World War I, Latin America also became important to the industrial powers of the northern hemisphere, as a major provider of the raw materials which they so desperately needed for their industrial plants. This meant that Latin American nations now occupied more of the center world stage, and both Latin Americans and others began to examine their political institutions more critically than before. The Wilsonian rhetoric of self-determination and democracy, coupled with this critical self- and other-examination, was one of the earlier examples of the demonstration effect, in which political, social, and economic institutions and mores in one society are put on display for members of other societies to examine.[4] What all this meant was that the old elites, who had governed most of the Latin American nations since independence in the early nineteenth century, became increasingly discredited in the eyes of many of their citizens. In Lipset's vocabulary, they lost their legitimacy, or their un-questioned right to rule, on the basis of blood lines, economic primacy, or even natural selection.[5].

It should be emphasized that this change in Latin American societies was part of a world-wide phenomenon. The inter-war period was a time of escalating social mobilization in the Middle East, Asia, and even Europe. The spectacle of a slight, stooped Vietnamese student named Ho Chi Minh, inquiring if President Wilson would see him concerning independence for Viet Nam, exemplifed some of the nationalist currents unleashed in Asia. In the Middle East, the twin nationalisms of Zionism and Arab nationalism also burgeoned as a result of World War I. Latin American nationalism and social mobilization were no exceptions to this historical trend. The new types of mobilizational dictatorship described above were partial results of these forces.

A third type of political leadership brought beginning democratic government to some Latin American nations. These democracies were, in most cases, only partial, and contained many inconsistencies. In several Latin American countries, however, major democratic leaders emerged during the years after World War I. Again, as in the case of the dictatorships, the results of these experiments in democracy were decidedly mixed in terms of political party development and resultant social cohesion. The Mexican experiment, and the development of the PNR (later the PRM and then the PRI) under Plutarco Calles has led to the creation of one of the most highly institutionalized political parties in the world, with a great deal of social cohesion in that country. In Venezuela the young democratically-minded leaders of "The Generation of '28" created the two mass-based political parties--AP and COPEI--in that country. Victor Raul Haya de la Torre and APRA in Peru, although not as successful in gaining power as the parties in Mexico and Venezuela, were also influenced by the winds of democracy and social mobilization which swept through Latin America after World War I.

Latin American politics in the inter-war period were characterized largely by the three types of govern-ment described above. To be sure, there were variants.

There always are in Latin America, and this is one
reason why the area continues to be a fascinating one
for political scientists. However, as indicated in
Table 1, almost all Latin American governments between
the two world wars fit into a typology constituted of
traditional dictatorships, mobilizational dictatorships,
and beginning (or incomplete) democracies.

TABLE 1

Traditional Dictatorships
    Guatemala
    El Salvador
    Honduras
    Nicaragua
    Panama
    Venezuela (to 1935)
    Ecuador
    Peru
    Cuba
    Dominican Republic
    Haiti
    Paraguay
    Bolivia

Mobilizational Dictatorship
    Brazil

Beginning Democracy
    Mexico
    Costa Rica
    Argentina (to 1930)
    Colombia
    Chile
    Uruguay

Although it is doubtful that they ever intended to
do so, some of the traditional dictators founded parties
that outlived the dictator. The Partido Dominicano in
the Dominican Republic, founded by Trujillo as his
personal political vehicle, was disbanded in 1961
shortly after the dictator's death, but was reconsti-
tuted in all but name by Joaquin Balaguer in 1966. On
the other hand, Machado and Batista in Cuba, Ubico in
Guatemala, Martinez in El Salvador, and Carias in
Honduras failed to produce any lasting political institutions.

As Table 1 indicates, mobilizational dictators were
still a rare breed in Latin America. In Brazil the
Partido Trabalhista Brasileira outlasted its founder,
Getulio Vargas.

The democrats (or, better, the quasi-democrats)
also produced some institutionalized political parties.
Betancourt and Caldera in Venezuela have been discussed,

as has Calles in Mexico. Although Calles has not been portrayed as a great democrat, as have the Venezuelans (and in fact even within Mexico Calles usually receives bad press), he belongs in this group for two reasons: first, we are interested in results in terms of political party development and second, Calles was operating within a more or less democratic framework (even though his intentions may have been less than honorable).

Perhaps the greatest democrat of them all, Jose Batlle y Ordoñez of Uruguay, was the most conscious creator of political institutions. The story of Batlle and the Blanco party of Uruguay has been told many times, and even though Uruguay has succumbed to the pressures of the 1970s and has become another nation governed by the bureaucratic military the Blancos (and the Colorados) for many years provided stability to Uruguayan politics. The democrats also produced negative results. The most mercurial, perplexing maddening democrat in Latin America during the period was, of course, Hipólito Yrigoyen in Argentina. Yrigoyen was the man with the greatest potential to affect Latin American politics, not only in Argentina, but throughout the hemisphere. This was so because at the time Argentina, not Brazil or Mexico, was the leader of the Latin American nations. One of the largest countries in the hemisphere, the only truly modern country in Latin America, Argentina in the twenties and thirties played the role that Mexico and Brazil have played in Latin America since the end of World War II. Yrigoyen, ultimately, failed miserably in his long relationship with the Union Civica Radical and this failure set the stage for the re-entry of the military into Argentine politics in 1930, and the subsequent continuing decline in social cohesion in that country.

Some of the democrats operated under much less favorable conditions than did Batlle, or Yrigoyen. Betancourt and Caldera in Venezuela and Ramon Grau San Martin in Cuba all faced the tremendous obstacle of having to organize and maintain political coalitions under the not-too-avuncular gaze of a dictatorship. Perhaps the most difficult task of organization and development was that of Victor Raul Haya de la Torre in Peru. Haya was faced not with a personalist dictator such as Gomez in Venezuela or Machado and Batista in Cuba, but with the implacable hostility of the Peruvian army. What this meant was that Haya's party, the Alianza Popular Revolucionaria Americana (APRA), could not look forward to an end to the enmity of those who ruled society. The Peruvian military in the 1920s and 1930s was, in a sense, the forerunner of the bureaucratic military of today in Latin America; and it is no accident that one of the foremost examples of this "new" type of military dictatorship existed in Peru until quite recently. For APRA and Haya, then, the death or removal of a <u>caudillo</u> could not signal the possibility of new beginnings and new opportunities as it did for the democrats in Venezuela. The Cuban democrats were faced with yet another situation, the demise of one <u>caudillo</u> (Machado) rapidly gave rise to another (Batista), so that the interregnum was simply too short to allow the democrats to take advantage of the momentary change. The situation in Cuba was further complicated by the alleged existence of a "super" <u>caudillo</u>--the United States. Several reputable historians have alleged that both Machado and Batista were, in effect, not in control of their own fortunes; but rather they relied for their ultimate authority upon the overwhelming economic, political, and social power of the United States.[6] In effect, the Cuban democrats could not rid themselves of their <u>caudillo</u> any more than the Peruvians, and their <u>caudillo</u> was as implacably opposed to the establishment of truly democratic government as was the Peruvian military.[7] Thus, political groups in Peru and Cuba were faced with a situation different from that in other Latin American nations: an impersonal <u>caudillo</u>, opposed to the development of most types of political expression (of which political parties were a part); but more ominously, a <u>caudillo</u> who refused to die or go away.

Political Parties in Latin America

Not much attention has been paid to the formation and development of political parties in Latin America. James MacGregor Burns, in his otherwise masterly study of leadership, simply states that "The new leaderships that emerged from tension points to change and conflict (in the developing nations) were largely controlled by ineluctable circumstances in shaping new party and other institutions."[8] Maurice Duverger, in his classic work on political parties, concentrates almost entirely on the parliamentary and group origins of parties within the European setting.[9] Other works concentrate almost entirely on the environmental aspects of party development in the developing nations and ignore the problem of institutional decay.

In the Latin American countries discussed above, it is clear that political parties were formed at different times and under different circumstances. Some insights into this process have already been recorded by a number of authors who have studied the formation of political parties in individual nations.[10] However, little has been written concerning the comparative aspects of political party origin and development in Latin America or elsewhere in the Third World. Most of the literature on political parties consists of a great deal of theorizing on the role of political parties in that mysterious process called "political development"--never really defined, except in western terms. Almost all of these efforts, it appears, commit the major sin of political science: they are full of theories about political parties and their role in political development, but they do not bother to ascertain how the particular parties in the countries became institutionalized. In these studies, political parties usually appear full-blown as either institutionalized or personalist. Rarely, however, are we presented with an explanation of the crucial variables that explain their development (or decay), or with a discussion of the crucial historical elements in the origin and development of political parties.[11]

This is, perhaps, why the works on party development in one country, although limited to the history of one political party (or at least one party system) are so helpful and illuminating. Some attempt to understand how and why political parties develop has been made by authors like Martz, Hofstadter, and others.[12] We begin to understand the interplay of history and personality on political party development, and we begin to see why (most of these books are success stories) the party system in the United States emerged as it did, or why Acción Democrática grew to be a strong party in Venezuela. A major fault of these histories is that, although they are full of facts, and insights can be gained by a discerning reader, there is little explicit theorizing either about the development of political parties or about their relationship with the larger society in which they operate. They are somewhat amorphous, a bit like flesh without the skeletal framework of theory to give it form. On the other hand, the theories concerning political party genesis and development resemble nothing so much as the skeleton without the flesh of understanding.

How are political parties formed and, more importantly, how do they become institutionalized? Several theories have been suggested, most inclusively by Joseph LaPalombara and Myron Weiner in their essay, "The Origin and Development of Political Parties."[13] These authors survey three types of theories concerning the creation and development of parties: so-called institutional theories which focus on the interrelationship between political parties and parliaments (primarily in the European context), theories which relate party development to historical crises in societies, and theories which relate party development to the modernization process.

LaPalombara and Weiner both admit, however, that the primarily institutional explanation of the development of political parties (that they arise either within the Parliament or outside the Parliament in oppositional groups) has little or no relevance to what they call

"the developing areas."[14]   This is, by and large,
the case with Latin American political parties. They
were not formed by groups within normally constituted
parliaments, although the <u>Blancos</u> in Uruguay formed and
developed during a period of both legislative and executive ascendance by groups supporting Batlle. And of
course, Batlle himself was a strong believer in a strong
legislature, so that a good part of the history of the
<u>Blancos</u> is related to the Uruguayan legislature. More
strictly speaking, however, the <u>Blancos</u> came into
existence through the personality of one man, who was
determined to alter the Uruguayan political system, and
who saw the creation of a political party as the
necessary means to this altering process.

   The second major theory concerning the creation and
development of political parties is that parties are
created and then develop in response to (or in their
turn create) crisis situations in the political system.
The crises of legitimacy, integration, and participation are given as the three major crises which have,
historically, been associated with the creation and or
development of political parties. Legitimacy, or the
question of who should rule, has been associated with
the rise of parties in Europe, especially at the times
when absolute monarchical rule came into question.
Parties provided some of the answer to the crisis of
legitimacy, in that they usually conferred some legitimacy on the new groups, be they nobles or commoners,
who moved into the role of governing elite. The crisis
of integration, or of molding a nation out of hetero-
geneous groups, is also commonly associated with the
development of parties, most recently in the one-party
systems of Africa and Asia after World War II. Finally,
the crisis of participation, or the question of who
should elect the rulers, has been associated with the
broader process of modernization occurring in all of the
non-western areas of the world. As people become
socially mobilized, demands on political systems
increase. One major demand, not normally heretofore
made, is for some say by the masses in the election of
their political leaders. Historically, one way of
meeting this demand has been through the creation of
political parties, which either actually provide the
participation being demanded, or are used as a
smokescreen for continued dominance by either an old or
a new elite. LaPalombara and Weiner conclude, after a
considerable survey of the literature on the subject,
that

> It would thus appear that it is the occurence
> of political crises of systemic magnitude at a
> point in time when sufficient modernization has
> taken place to provide conditions for party de-
> velopment that causes parties to emerge.[15]

Thus far, we have been alternately criticizing and utilizing LaPalombara and Weiner almost exclusively. The reason for this is that they have provided the best synthesis of most recent writings on political party development. Ultimately, however, they do not provide a satisfactory explanation concerning party genesis and development. Their analysis is unidimensional, in that they do not consider the problem of institutional decay, nor do they go beyond the environmental factors in party development. These factors are important, and they provide the regularities social scientists love, but they are far from the entire story.

Among major works dealing with political parties is the seminal work by Maurice Duverger. Entitled simply Political Parties, the book deals in its introduction with the origins of political parties. Although the treatment is rather summary, Duverger does lay out the traditional methods of party formation (e.g. parliamentary groupings faced with the necessity of dealing with a mobilized electorate, or extra-parliamentary groups intent upon changing the system or at least resting control from the "ins") and contrasts these with some of the non-European paths to party development. Further, Duverger presents some slight analysis of the differences among political parties depending on their origin.[16]

In Parties and Politics, Avery Leiserson analyzes not only the institutional but the psychological origins of political, parties. He also provides us with a great deal more historical insight into the origin and development of political parties than do most other writers on the subject. In summing up, Leiserson states:

> Political parties, or perhaps we should say politics, originate in the factional cleavages of personal and group interests in society, which seek to protect and promote these interests by controlling the formal structure of public authority. As long as the justifying symbols and power practices in the political system are rigidly based upon custom and authoritarian absolutism from above, political parties in the modern sense cannot develop beyond the form of factional minorities conspiring to displace or control the existing holders of power. With the mass expansion of political participation to include all or most citizens through the suffrage, the factional groups in society are compelled to extend their organization to acquire a mass following in the electorate and to connect these followings by psychological and institutional forms of representation with the occupants of executive, legislative and administrative office.[17]

Leiserson goes on to discuss the evolution of political parties: parties develop "an autonomous leadership and power base" which they use to contend with other centers of social and economic power in the society. Unless they opt for the revolutionary route, parties must also form mutual pacts with interest groups, the media, and the bureaucracy.[18] Parties also perform functions, such as encouraging party loyalty and political participation, controlling the nomination process, and organizing the government, and the performance of these functions enhances their possibilities of survival. The relative success in performing these functions (relative not only to other parties, but to other competing groups within society) will either strengthen or weaken the party.[19]

We have discussed and quoted from Avery Leiserson's book at some length because he begins to do what is necessary to understand the successes and failures of political parties. Leiserson makes many of the points emphasized in LaPalombara and Weiner, most importantly that political parties come into existence when expansion of the suffrage or some other systemic crisis forces groups or cabals to begin to appeal to the mass public, and that the growth of political parties is due primarily to the way in which those parties meet the challenges hurled at them by the society in which they operate. Still, even the best of theory books do not provide the historical understanding necessary to undergird their theories. What this book proposes to do is to provide a body of knowledge about the growth (and decay) of political parties and their relation to national development.

There are several works which examine the rise of political parties within individual nations. In one of the best of these Richard Hofstadter chronicles the rise of the party system within the United States from 1780 to 1840; and demonstrates how, in a system whose leaders were originally opposed to political parties as creators of factionalism, political parties began to develop as a consequence of the exact conditions described by Leiserson in his book:

> The proportion of eligible popular voters was also growing. In these years the states of the eastern seaboard were liberalizing their suffrage requirements to a point that allowed virtual universal manhood suffrage, and the new states of the west were entering with minimal limitations. By 1824 nearly all adult white males could vote in presidential elections outside of Virginia, Rhode Island, and Louisiana. Voter apathy had prevailed in non-competitive states during the interval between party systems and in the ill-contested presidential

election of 1816 and the non-contested one of
1820. But the renewal of keen personal
rivalries in 1824 persuaded politicians that
there was an increasing potential electorate,
available to be won by well-organized parties.
The return of party competition once set in
motion, began to feed upon itself, as strenuous
efforts to reach the enlarged electorate began
to pay off.[20]

Hofstadter is saying, of course, that the growth of
political parties in the United States was due to the
extension of the suffrage, which made it necessary for
the quarreling groups of American political leaders at
the time to appeal to these broader constituencies. Why
was this necessary? Hofstadter is explicit:

Finally, new political conditions diminished
the power of old elites. The new efforts to
reach broad electorates, the increasing use of
political "staging,"...required more and more
time and devotion, and a greater willingness to
approach the common man on his own terms. It
therefore put a premium on the efforts of men
who were willing to devote all, or almost all,
of their time to politics, and who did not
expect leadership to fall to them as a matter
of deference, celebrity, or wealth. Where
political leadership in the time of Hamilton
and Jefferson was a thing that almost automatically fell to the gentry, it now fell
increasingly to men who were prepared to make a
vocation of politics.... It was not surprising that such men would have, in addition to
their new problems and new agencies, a different feeling about political life, and that they
should develop new ideas about the role of the
party.[21]

The rule that political parties will not appear
until there is a broad extension of the suffrage is not
universal, however. John Martz, in his history of
Acción Democrática in Venezuela chronicles the rise of a
modern political party during a period of intermittent,
but powerful, dictatorships in that country. Much of
the organizing work of the party was done under difficult conditions:

As of 1964, fully ten of the Acción Democrática's twenty-three years of existence had been
spent in exile. And for the party founders
whose political activism dated back to 1928,
twenty-one of the thirty-six years to follow
were lived in political exile, almost all of it

outside Venezuela proper.[22]

In fact, after 1936, the Venezuelan electorate was constricted more than it had been earlier. In that year, a new constitution perpetuated a system of indirect election of national officials while constricting the electorate. Until that year, all males over twenty-one had been allowed to vote for municipal councilmen and for state legislators. These officials in turn elected the national legislators, who then elected the chief executive. The 1936 constitution continued this system of indirect election, but restricted the vote to literate men over the age of twenty-one. In Venezuela, with an illiteracy rate of over seventy per cent, this shrank the electorate tremendously. The subsequent dictatorships, first of Lopez Contreras in the 1930s and early 1940s, and then of the army and Perez Jimenez in the late 1940s and the 1950s, made any further question of an expanding electorate ludicrous. Yet, Acción Democrática not only managed to survive, but also to organize throughout the nation.

In Chile, the rise of the Radical Party in the 1920s was accompanied by increased participation by the masses.[23] Yet at the same time, there was no vast increase in the electorate. Women and illiterate males were prohibited from voting until the 1950s. The rise of the Radical party and the electoral victories of Alessandri during the 1920s were accompanied by increased participation of those already enfranchised, but new electors did not enter the political life of Chile until much later in its history. The caudillos of the time--Trujillo, Somoza, and especially Vargas--did depart from previous dictatorial tradition in Latin America, in that they all, to some degree, tried to enlist popular support for their dictatorships through the medium of the political party. Nevertheless, electorates remained relatively constricted in all these countries and, of course, the vote was meaningless, even when it was exercised.

Although development of political parties in Latin America does not appear to have been a result of an expanded electorate (at least in most cases), if we substitute the broader term of social mobilization for expanded electorate we may come closer to the real environmental reason for political party development. It is simply that all political leaders in Latin America, whether they were caudillos or democrats (or something in between) had to take into account the increased demands for at least the illusion of political participation which resulted from increases in literacy, urbanizaiton, media, and all the other factors which tend to transform societies from traditional to modern. Thus, societal factors operating in Latin America in the 1920s and 1930s created the necessary but not sufficient conditions for the origin and development of political parties. The overlooked catalyst, present in some countries but not in others, was political leadership.

Political Leadership and Party Origins

As we have seen, writings on political parties tend to concentrate on the environmental variables associated with the genesis and development of those parties. Parties are formed because conditions in a particular society are "ripe" for that formation, and parties develop within those societies because of changed conditions in those societies. There is little within the literature of the discipline that deals with the personal variable of leadership associated with the founding of political institutions. Yet, it is a major thesis of this work that this personal element is crucial in the successes and failures of party development in Latin America. As Harold Lasswell stated years ago, "Political Science without biography is a form of taxidermy."[24] Lasswell goes on to drive home his (and my) point:

It is no news that "Leadership" is an important variable in predicting the course of events, but the standard treatises on politics have next to nothing to offer about the traits of various kinds of agitators and organizers, and nothing to say about the kinds of experiences out of which these differences arise.[25]

Writing some thirty-six years later, Fred Greenstein made the same point: "There is a great deal of political activity which can be explained adequately only by taking account of the personal characteristics of the actors involved."[26] Greenstein then tackles the question of why most political scientists are reluctant to deal with psychological matters. His reasons are many and cogent, and underline the fact that the discipline has concentrated almost exclusively on environmental factors to explain political phenomena, including the origin and development of political parties.

Yet, the most cursory examination of the course of political parties in Latin America suggests strongly that Lasswell and Greenstein are correct. One need only look at the case of Yrigoyen and the Unión Cívica Radical in Argentina to witness a compelling argument in favor of the importance of the personal factor in the history of political parties. The facts are that, on the surface at least, all of the environmental conditions described by Leiserson, Duverger, LaPalombara and

Weiner, Hofstadter, and others as favorable to the development of political parties were present in Argentina
in the 1920s. Argentina was fast becoming a middle-
class nation, with almost universal manhood suffrage, so
the Argentine electorate was expanding rapidly. At the
same time, the old elite who had controlled Argentina
politics until World War I were rapidly becoming discredited. Conditions for the development of a strong
political party representing these new groups in
Argentine society seemed propitious, and indeed they
were. It also appeared that, from 1916 to 1928, the
Unión Cívica Radical would become that party. However,
between 1928 and 1930, personality triumphed over the
environment, in one of the great tragedies of Latin
American politics, Yrigoyen the great leader of the UCR,

> ...gave more and more signs of his physical and
> mental decline. He...neglected public affairs,
> was capricious and irritable, and held himself
> aloof, almost as a hermit, from national pro-
> blems and presidential duties. During his
> first year, this made little difference, since
> Argentina was such a marvelous social organism
> that she flourished irrespective of politics.
> In October, 1929, however, the Wall Street cat-
> astrophe plunged the world of international
> trade into disorder, and Argentina was one of
> the first countries to feel the effects. The
> depression threw into relief her social fis-
> sures and the flaws in her structure. Chal-
> lenged by a vast economic crisis, Yrigoyen's
> government practically disintegrated.[27]

Those who stress environmental factors will
undoubtedly seize upon the depression as the "cause" of
the decline of the UCR in Argentina. But the same depression was hitting with equal force elsewhere in Latin
America, and in other countries party leaders were controlling the situation and becoming stronger as a result
of the crisis. The major explanatory variable of these
instances--one of the virtual disintegration of a
political party and the other the strengthening of a
party--seems to be a factor of political leadership. In
Argentina, Hipólito Yrigoyen was old, unbalanced, and
weary, and was unable to respond to the challenge he and
the party he led faced. In other countries leaders were
ready for the challenge of economic hard times, and
benefited from the challenge. In one country, political leadership was used to develop a strong political
party. In another country, political leadership did not
exploit the crisis to further develop a political party.
Instead, the leader became ever more personalist in his
rule, ever less mindful of the historical mission en-
trusted to him by recent political history, and as a

result that country plunged into the sea of militarism, violence, and repression from which it has only recently emerged.

The question, of course, is why did Yrigoyen fail in Argentina while others succeeded elsewhere. Why was Calles in Mexico able to "lift his individual patient-hood to the level of a universal one and...try to solve for all what he could not solve for himself."?[28] Why on the other hand did Yrigoyen fall into the Lasswellian pattern of displacing "private affects upon public objects."?[29] As Dankwart Rustow has stated:

> The difference may well coincide with that between leaders like Hitler or Wilson who, after spectacular successes, destroy them-selves and their work, and those like Luther or Gandhi, whose works endure.[30]

This book, then is concerned with the development of political parties and their effect upon the pax civica of several Latin American nations. The rise of these parties, out of the political conditions of Latin American states in the 1920s and 1930s, has been a major variable in determining the level of social cohesion of these nations. At the same time, however, this work is also concerned with the psychology of the political leaders who were involved in the political events of Latin America in the inter-war period. For it is a major thesis of this work that the variable of political leadership played an important, if not overwhelming role in determining which political parties developed and which did not. A further sub-thesis is that there are certain regularities of political leadership which will explain the difference between Yrigoyen and Alessandri, between Betancourt and Vargas, between Calles and Grau San Martin. In short, the political mind-set or political personality of these individuals will explain in large measure their successes and failures as political leaders whose initial successes either endured or turned to ashes.

The Wellsprings of Political Leadership

What is it that makes a leader? Are political leaders different from leaders in other walks of life? Can we find any regularities of leadership, or are we condemned to continually write biographies, unrelated one to another, of great men and women? This book does not pretend to examine all types of leadership at all times. Nor does it aspire to a study of all types of political leadership. What we hope to do is to examine leaders that Lasswell called "Administrators," as opposed to his "Agitators" and "Theorists." We are interested, not in the revolutionary leader endowed with Max Weber's charismatic authority, but rather with Weber's second type of authority, the rational-legal leader who, in Weber's cycle, supplants the initial, charismatic leader.[31] James MacGregor Burns calls this second type of leadership "transactional," and includes in this group leaders of opinion, group leaders, party leaders, and legislative and executive leaders.[32] These are, of course, pure types, and Lasswell includes in his typology "composite" types, who partake of the combined characteristics of administrator, agitator, and theorist. Certainly, most of the people we will investigate are composites of at least two of Lasswell's categories, but probably the institution builders we are looking for are closer to the administrators than to any other type.

In a way, it is relatively easy to classify leaders into typologies. The difficult part is to determine (a) why certain people become leaders, and (b) why certain leaders create enduring institutions while others do not. Although there is a plethora of works on the subject of leadership, none presents any compelling evidence as to the wellsprings of leadership. Nowhere is this better illustrated than in Burns' work cited above, which is a recent compendium of the various theories of leadership. Burns states:

> We will note...that authoritarian rulers can emerge from relatively benign circumstances and democratic leaders from less benign ones. This will only enhance our sense of humility, complexity, and mystery (useful intellectual inhibitions in the exploration of leadership).[33]

Leadership is, then, in Burns' words, "intensely individual and personal," and any study of its origins must be, at best, speculative. At the outset, we must regard as useful the theories of Erikson, Lasswell, Rustow, Maslow, and others.[34] At the same time, however, we must keep an open mind as to the "crucibles of political leadership". Are potential political leaders impelled by a combination of displacement and rationalization, as Lasswell suggests, or are leaders formed by successfully dealing with Erikson's "identity crisis" in early life? Or, as Lorenz and other ethnologists suggest, is leadership biologically determined? Perhaps the best corrective to exclusive dependence on any one theory of leadership formation is Burns' observation that "the force that may be the most important in shaping most leaders..." is learning. By learning we mean a broad process whereby the individual learns "from experience,...from people,...from successes and failures,...from leaders and followers..."[35] What is suggested here is that a complex of biological, psychological, and social forces combines to produce leaders, and that we must examine all of these forces in order to begin to glimpse the seemingly mysterious process of leadership creation.

This book, however, is not ultimately concerned with the question of political leadership in general. Rather, we are looking for a particular type of political leader; the person who creates and builds institutions (as well as his counterpart, the destroyer of institutions). Even more specifically, we are asking questions about leaders and political parties in Latin America. Our early hypothesis is that a type of "bureaucratic leader" has been responsible for the creation and subsequent development of institutionalized political parties. Our counter-hypothesis is that the traditional charismatic leader has generally either failed to develop these parties, or has contributed to the disintegration of parties once they have developed.

Bureaucratic leader is a new term, at least in the context used here. We are not speaking of the leader of a bureaucracy but rather of a certain type of political leader, usually in an executive position, who finds his continued control over the political process blocked by his relative lack of charismatic appeal, either to the masses of people or to a ruling clique within the country, as was the historic custom in Latin America. This person is contrasted with the charismatic leader who rules by force of personality, all the while making the political deals necessary. Both leaders want political power, but each must seek his own path to that power, within the limitations set by the type of leadership personality developed during a lifetime. The bureaucratic leader finds it difficult to change. His biological inheritance, his psychological conditioning, his learning experiences, the forces of society--have all combined to produce his political personality. So, too, with the charismatic leader. Individual leadership comes easy to him, and the need to build institutions to control the political process is lacking. Each type, when confronted with a political situation demanding leadership, will respond differently, and the different responses have had (and will continue to have) profound influences on the course of political history. Some leaders have succeeded in developing long-lasting and institutionalized political parties, while others have failed in the attempt.

Political Parties and Social Cohesion

The terms "success" and "failure" have been repeatedly used in the context of developing political institutions. An adequate definition of these amorphous terms is vital, because for many years in the lexicon of

comparative politics the term "development" substituted
for success, and development was almost never defined by
the people writing about that political process. Development (or success) was assumed to mean the creation of
a political system closely approximating the models
found in North America and Western Europe, and almost no
consideration was given to the question of whether those
models were indeed, appropriate ones.[36] Further,
through the use of the term "democratic stability" many
authors fell into the trap of equating systems which
followed the form of western democracy with those
systems which embodied the spirit of true democratic
institutions.[37] Many of us remember listening to an
eminent political scientist report on the Viet Nam elections of 1968, indicating that those elections were, in
essence, democratic, as they had followed the form of
western-style elections.[38] No matter that the
climate of fear and reek of moral decay in South Viet
Nam made these elections a farce. No matter, indeed,
whether these elections had any meaning whatsoever for
the people who sullenly participated in them. The
important point for the reporter (and for the U. S.
government) was that the form had been followed. So we
are not interested in this book in whether or not a
particular country has followed the form of representative democracy, nor are we interested in whether that
country is "stable." For years, political scientists
interested in political development trumpeted stability
as something that was to be highly prized by developing
nations. The regime that could bring about political
stability was the regime that was successful (i.e. more
developed along the lines of the western model) than its
less stable contemporaries. Of course, the fallacy was
(and is) there. Brazil is stable (since 1964 no regime
change). Chile appears to be much more stable than
before 1973. Uruguay is stable. But the truth of the
matter is that this stability is brought about through
the massive use of repressive tactics by the government.
Thus, stability in these countries is a chimera, and
actually represents a great deal of potential instability that will manifest itself as soon as the repression
is removed. This is not to say that stability is all
bad--it isn't--but only that stability is not success,
at least in terms of the political good.

What then, if neither the democratic form nor
political stability represents success, is success in
terms of the good political system? In an earlier
effort, a colleague and I have advanced the term "social
cohesion" as almost synonymous with success. Social
cohesion was defined as a relative absence of both
political violence and repression. In this work we
recognized that certain forms of economic and social
oppression might make outright repression by the government unnecessary. As Oscar Lewis has demonstrated, the

culture of poverty is generally a rather conservative ambience, and the reasons are not difficult to fathom.[39] People with empty stomachs who spend most of their waking hours foraging for enough to keep from starving simply do not have either the energy or the inclination to engage in revolutionary activities. Although it might not qualify as repression, the age-old syndrome of substituting circuses for bread may very well affect people's inclinations toward violence. Every year, during the bicycle race known as La Vuelta a Colombia, practically all political activity in that country comes to a standstill. People forget their political hurts for a week and concentrate on a bicycle race. Although there is no documentation for it, it appears that a steady diet of Yo Quiero a Lucy might very well dampen the revolutionary ardor of poor people in Latin American nations. The effect of TV, sports events and divertissments in general on political activity is poorly understood. Given the caveat of indeterminacy, however, it appears that the concept of social cohesion may be about as close as a political scientist can get to an operationalization of the successful political system. That is, those systems with high levels of social cohesion (and consequently low levels of violence and repression) are successful and those with low levels of social cohesion (and consequently high levels of violence and repression) are unsuccessful.

Now that we have advanced the concept of social cohesion, we should ask, what are the societal conditions (variables) that are associated with high levels of social cohesion. In the study alluded to previously, one independent variable stood out as strongly, positively, and continually associated with social cohesion. This variable was institutionalization of certain elements of society, primarily the political parties. Where political parties are strong in Latin America, repression tends to be low. Where political parties are weak, repression tends to be high. Where political parties are strong violence tends to be low. Where parties are weak, violence tends to be high. One of the crucial determinants of the level of social cohesion in Latin America, then, is the strength of political parties. Briefly, an institutionalized political party is (a) one that has lasted a long time, (b) one that has survived changes in its leadership, and (c) one that produces political leaders from within the party rather than relying on outside personalities to bring the party electoral success.[40] Examples abound: The Democratic Party of the United States, the oldest political party in the world, is an institutionalized political party. The Republican Party of the United States is also institutionalized, but because it seems to rely more on outside personalities to bring it electoral success (the Eisenhower phenomenon), it is probably less institutionalized than are the Democrats. The Conservative and Labour Parties in the United Kingdom are institutionalized, as is the Communist Party of the Soviet Union. In Latin America, the PRI in Mexico, the Conservatives and Liberals in Colombia, AD and COPEI in Venezuela, the URD in Costa Rica, and the Peronistas in Argentina all exhibit varying degrees of institutionalization. In fact, it is wrong to say that Party A is institutionalized and Party B is not. Institutionalization, like most political phenomena, is not an either-or proposition, but must be treated as lying on a continuum, with parties at one end being more institutionalized than the parties at the other end of the continuum. Thus, a continuum of political party institutionalization in Latin America might look like this:

Figure 1

More institutionalization   Less institutionalization

$\longleftarrow$——————————————————————$\longrightarrow$

PRI (Mexico)
        AD and COPEI (Venezuela)
                Liberals (Colombia)
                        Accion Popular (Peru)

What we are saying, then, is that there are ways of ascertaining the degree of institutionalization of political parties, and that the degree to which these parties are institutionalized is vital to the political peace of the country in which they operate.

In order to continue our logical argument, we must now restate an earlier hypothesis: Institutionalized political parties in some Latin American countries are institutionalized not because of foreign aid or because of anything that has been done or not been done by the political elite of the Latin American countries or of the United States since World War II, but because in the 1920s and the 1930s events and political leaders concatenated to create and develop these parties. Put simply, Plutarco Calles has more to do with the institutionalization of the PRI in Mexico (and consequently the relative social cohesion that nation enjoys) than does any Mexican leader or United States policy since World War II. Conversely, Hipólito Yrigoyen is responsible for the relative lack of social cohesion in Argentina-- more so than the Peronists, the Montoneros, the ERP, the gorilas, or United States policy toward that country. Again history is not fixed, and of course recent events, policies and personalities have had an effect on current situations. However the political stability in Mexico or the chaos in Argentina was largely determined forty to fifty years ago, by people and events of that earlier time. If this hypothesis is correct the implications are substantial. First, it means that there is not much anyone can do, at least in the short term, about the current lack of social cohesion in many Latin American nations. Their political course was fixed a half century ago, and they simply do not have the political institutions necessary to bring political peace. Second, it is doubtful that any short-term developmental efforts such as the late lamented Caribbean Basin Initiative will have much effect on the politics of any Latin American country. This is so simply because (as this and many other studies amply demonstrate) political parties cannot be formed overnight. Their gestation takes time, and in almost all of the cases we will examine here, the political parties that eventually brought a modicum of social cohesion to some Latin American countries were formed wholly through the efforts of the nationals of those countries. The lesson for planners and diplomats concerned with the political future of Latin America is clear: foreign aid, technical assistance, study missions, and all the rest are in themselves useful, but no one should expect any short or medium term political results from these efforts. They simply cannot overcome the tremendous inertia of political events that took place long ago, but which have long-term and decisive effects on the politics of the nations where the events took place. Such a realization might induce some slight humility in policies long characterized by their hubris.

If the formation or disintegration of political parties capable of dominating or at least controlling the political process in Latin American nations is of such import, and if factors of personality and leadership are of considerable importance in determining the course of development of these parties, then an examination of the lives of some of the people involved in this process should be instructive, not only as a clue to the past and present, but also as an insight into the future. If we can determine why that unlikely political hero, Plutarco Calles, succeeded in Mexico while a much more impressive politician (Getulio Vargas) failed in Brazil, then we may be able to look at the present political leadership in Latin America (and elsewhere) and apply some of the lessons learned. Hopefully, an examination of the interrelationships between political leadership and political party development will uncover some of the regularities of political leadership associated with both success and failure in this crucial political endeavor. What are these regularities associated with either success or failure? Only a detailed examination of the lives of these individuals, as well as the times in which they lived, can provide the answer.

Notes

1. Tad Szulc, Twilight of the Tyrants (New York: Praeger, 1959).
2. The best study of Trujillo (and arguably the best study of any caudillo) is Robert Crassweller, Trujillo: Life and Times of a Caribbean Dictator (New York: MacMillan, 1966).
3. Donald M. Dozer, Latin America: An Interpretive History (New York: McGraw-Hill, 1962), 504.
4. Cyril E. Black, The Dynamics of Modernization (New York: Harper and Row, 1966), 54-61.
5. See Seymour Marin Lipset, Political Man (New York: Doubleday, 1960).
6. Luis E. Aguilar, Cuba: 1933 (Ithaca, N. Y.; Cornell University Press, 1972); and Hugh Thomas, Cuba: The Pursuit of Freedom (New York: Harper and Row, 1971), 606.
7. Thomas, 627.
8. James MacGregor Burns, Leadership (New York: Harper and Row, 1978), 335.
9. Maurice Duverger, Political Parties (New York: John Wiley and Sons, 1963), xxxvii.
10. See John D. Martz, Acción Democrática (Princeton: Princeton University Press, 1965); Robert E. Scott, Mexican Government in Transition (Urbana Illinois, University of Illinois Press, 1964); and Maria Antonieta Benejam, "Partido Revolucionario Institucional: Proceso de la Institucionalizacion de un Partido Politico," Unpublished thesis for Licenciatura en Sociologia, Universidad Nacional Autonoma de Mexico, 1972.
11. In addition to the works cited in the introduction additional first-rate works on political parties include: Giovanni Sartori, Parties and Party Systems (New York: Cambridge University Press, 1976); Sigmund Neumann (ed.), Modern Political Parties (Chicago: University of Chicago Press, 1956); and Kay Lawson, The Comparative Study of Political Parties (New York: St. Martin's Press, 1976).
12. Martz, Chapter 1. Richard Hofstadter, The Idea of a Party System (Berkeley: University of California Press, 1969), 209-210.
13. Joseph LaPalombara and Myron Weiner, "The Origins and Development of Political Parties," in Joseph LaPalombara and Myron Weiner (eds.), Political Parties and Political Development (Princeton: Princeton University Press, 1966).
14. Ibid., 12.
15. Ibid., 15.
16. Duverger, xxxvi.
17. Avery Leiserson, Parties and Party Politics (New York: Alfred A. Knopf, 1958), 79-80.
18. Ibid., 80.

28

19. Ibid., 81.
20. Hofstadter, 210.
21. Ibid., 211.
22. Martz, 119.
23. Benejam, 10.
24. Harold Lasswell, Psychopathology and Politics (Chicago: University of Chicago Press, 1931), 1.
25. Ibid., 2.
26. Fred Greenstein, "The Impact of Personality on Politics: An Attempt to Clear Away the Underbrush," American Political Science Review 61 (1967), 629.
27. John E. Fagg, Latin America; A General History (New York: MacMillan Publishing Co., 1977), 470.
28. Erik Erikson, Young Man Luther (New York: Norton, 1962), 67.
29. Lasswell, 75-76.
30. Dankwart Rustow, Philosophers and Kings (New York: Brazilier, 1970), 231.
31. Michael Toth, The Theory of the Two Charismas (Washington: University Press of America, 1981), 107-114.
32. Burns, 123.
33. Ibid., 27.
34. Previously cited works of Erikson, Lasswell, and Rustow. Abraham Maslow, The Farther Reaches of Human Nature (New York: The Viking Press, 1971).
35. Burns, 63.
36. Perhaps the most popular and influential of a whole spate of "developmental" literature was Gabriel Almond and G. Bingham Powell, Comparative Politics: A Developmental Approach (Boston: Little, Brown, 1966).
37. Robert Dahl, Polyarchy, Participation, and Opposition (New Haven: Yale University Press, 1971).
38. Speech by J. Roland Pennock to the Annual Convention of the American Political Science Association, Washington, D.C., September, 1968.
39. Oscar Lewis, "The Culture of Poverty," Scientific American 215:16 (October, 1966), 21-25.
40. Ernest Duff and John McCamant, Violence and Repression in Latin America (New York: The Free Press, 1976), 103-107.

Part 2
The Successful Institution Builders

   Creators of institutions are rare in any ambience,
but this seems to be especially true in politics. Perhaps this lack of institution builders can be ascribed
to the politicians' inordinate love of and pursuit of
power for power's sake, as the original goals of politics have become lost to view in the modern age.[1]
Certainly, the modern definition of politics as the
quest for power (with no question as to the uses of
power) has become so commonplace as to become banal.[2]
Further, when one speaks of Latin American politics the
images that come immediately to mind are those of the
venal, grasping politician with no regard for the common
good, and with little sense of the future.[3]   Yet,
within this promising milieu various individuals have,
for disparate reasons, created enduring political
institutions. Their motives, as we shall see, were
varied and many times veiled, but the end result was the
same: The creation of an institutionalized political
party that in one form or another subsequently played a
major role in the ongoing political life of the nation.
Among these institution builders three incredibly
different men stand out: Plutarco Calles in Mexico,
Rafael Trujillo in the Dominican Republic, and Romulo
Betancourt in Venezuela. Each of these men founded or
developed a political party that subsequently played a
major role in bringing a modicum of political peace to
the nation. What we propose to do in this section is to
examine the lives and times of each of these apparently
dissimilar men to see if there were, in fact, any
commonalities that might explain the similar outcomes of
their efforts at institution building. Further, using
the concept of actor dispensability, we will tackle the
question of how these men, with their varying styles of
political leadership, all played a major role in the
political processes of their nations.

2
Plutarco Calles and the Formation of the Mexican PRI

By consensus, the most successful of the political parties created in Latin America in this century has been the Partido Revolucionario Institucional[1] of Mexico, which was founded in 1929 and which has successfully dominated the politics of Mexico from that year to the present. In spite of this conspicuous success, however, there have been no full-scale studies in English of the genesis and subsequent early institutionalization of the PRI. This chapter is an attempt to examine the development of the PRI within the various theories of party development outlined in Chapter I.

The most searching analysis of the development of the PRI is contained in an article by the Mexican sociologist Jose Luis Reyna. In writing about Mexican political developments of the 1920s, Reyna states:

> These indicators (economic growth, urbanization, industrialization, increased communication) taken together allow one to assume the validity of the hypothesis that, in effect, there was a certain economic dynamism in the decade. One can also suppose that this is the period during which the economic and production base began to move from the agricultural sector to the urban sector. And at the same time these structural changes were beginning to affect the political model that reigned in Mexico. It can be suggested, as a hypothesis, that these changes brought about, in some form, the redefinition of the basis of power of the Mexican state.
>
> It is in the middle of these conditions that the Partido Nacional Revolucionario emerges in 1929. Its founding seems to be a logical consequence that responded to the necessity of redefining a political model that was becoming more vulnerable to the types of changes that

were being generated within the socio-economic
structure of the country. In other words, the
political availability of diverse social
groups, especially of urban origin, would have
been able to question the type of system in
terms of the interests that each one of them
represented. The charismatic political model,
moreover, was showing signs of not being able
to absorb these interests.[2]

Although he is apparently alone in his analysis of
the formation of the PNR, Reyna follows in an ample
tradition of works by authors who have been concerned
with the more general question of the formation and
institutionalization of political parties. As we have
seen, LaPalombara and Weiner have suggested three types
of explanatory theories of political party creation and
institutionalization: the so-called institutional
theories, which relate party development to historical
crises in societies, and theories which relate party
development to the modernization process.[3] LaPalombara and Weiner state in their conclusion:

It would thus appear that it is the occurrence
of political crises of systemic magnitude at a
point in time when sufficient modernization has
taken place to provide conditions for party
development that causes political parties to
emerge.[4]

This is, by and large, true of Latin American parties.
The formation of the PNR, for example, occurred completely outside of any constituted parliament, as did
the formation of most other parties in the area.
    The theory that parties are created either in
response to crisis situations or to the modernization
process has relevance to Latin America. The crises of
legitimacy, integration, and participation which are
historically, the three major crises resulting from the
modernization process and which are associated with
party development, have all been felt in Latin America
at one time or another. The crisis of participation, or
who should elect the rulers, is the crisis to which
Reyna refers, in an oblique manner, in his article on
the Mexican PRI.
    A detailed study of the formation of the PNR in
Mexico leads one inescapably to the conclusion that,
while societal conditions may have provided the
necessary variable for party development, the crucial
element in the genesis of that party was political leadership. One needs only to compare the environmental
circumstances in Mexico and Argentina during the 1920s,
and then compare political party development in the two
countries during the same and subsequent periods, to

appreciate the central role played by political leadership. In both countries the environment was favorable
to the establishment of political parties, and in fact
the economic and social process of modernization was far
more advanced in Argentina than it was in Mexico.[5] In
Argentina, despite favorable environmental factors for
party development, Yrigoyen proceeded, during the last
years of the 1920s, to tear apart the Radical Party. At
the same time, in Mexico, Plutarco Elias Calles was
creating a party that ranks among the most institutionalized political parties in the world.[6]

The question, of course, for anyone interested in
politics is why did Calles in Mexico succeed in
exploiting the political crisis of 1928-1929 to develop
a political party, while Yrigoyen was moving in the
opposite direction? What is the type of political leadership associated with the development of political
institutions that outlive their founders? Why was
Calles able to create a lasting political institution in
Mexico, while seemingly more promising leaders in
equally propitious environmental conditions (Yrigoyen,
Grau San Martin in Cuba, Haya de la Torre in Peru,
Getulio Vargas in Brazil) fail to respond adequately to
similar situations in their countries?

The Environment

No man dominated twentieth century Mexican politics
for as long a period as did Plutarco Calles. The period
from the beginning of Calles' presidential term in 1924
to the end of the Maximato in 1934 was one first of
shared power with Álvaro Obregón and later of almost
total power, exerted behind the scenes, by Calles alone.
According to Edwin Lieuwen, "General Plutarco Calles was
the most durable political personality to emerge from
the Revolution. He dominated Mexican politics for a
decade."[7]

The decade of the 1920s was one of great
uncertainty for the future course of the Revolution of
1910. The proponents of a new order for Mexico had
succeeded militarily against those who wished to turn
the clock back to the Porfiriato. Moreover, some
political stability had been achieved. With the inauguration of Calles as president in 1924, the presidency
passed peacefully from one chief executive to another
for the first time in forty years, in spite of the
rebellion led by Adolfo de la Huerta, who wished to
succeed Obregón as president. The overt, warring phase
of the Revolution, which had characterized the years
from 1910 to 1920, was largely over, thanks in large
part to the political genius and charisma of Alvaro
Obregón. Nevertheless, serious political problems had
to be overcome if Mexico was to continue to experience a
deepening of the fragile political stability it had

begun to experience. Foremost among these was the problem of personalismo. There was no institutionalized method of choosing a new president. The generals still ruled and elections (1920, 1924, 1928) were still characterized by a great deal of interpersonal feuding and violence.[8]

Although political parties existed in Mexico during the 1920s, "almost all the States of the Republic were governed by caudillos and regional caciques. The caudillos and caciques of the towns and regions dominated the national panorama."[9] "In the State of Mexico in the electoral register of 1925 there were more than 200 parties, while in the Federal District there were 107; and in 1928 in the entire country there were 8,000 identifiable political parties."[10] In spite of Obregón's relative success in creating some type of political order in the country, the lack of any true political machinery for resolving conflicts and deciding upon new leadership was sorely apparent:

> All in all, this lack of broadly based and effective civilian parties produced an extremely unstable political situation, as coalitions formed and dissolved in response to the shifting ambitions of their members. The speed with which the various factions rose and fell betrays their lack of institutional basis, for although each party claimed to represent the Revolution, or some phase of it, behind each party lurked a personalist leader.[11]

As of 1924, such political peace as Mexico might enjoy seemed to rest on the continued survival of the two remaining national caudillos, Obregón and Calles, both from the State of Sonora, in northwest Mexico. Things remained that way for the next four years. There is a great deal of circumstantial evidence that the two men planned to continue their domination of Mexican politics by alternating the presidency. In 1928, Calles and Obregón had the 1917 Constitution changed in one of its key aspects. The cry of the original revolutionaries of Effective Suffrage and No Reelection was now changed (as was the Constitution) to Effective Suffrage and no Immediate Reelection, thus paving the way for Obregón's reelection to the presidency in 1928. The implicit understanding, of course, was that Calles would return as president after Obregón had served his term in office, and in this way the two Sonorans could dominate Mexican politics for some time to come.[12]

The most obvious problem with the arrangement was that it depended upon the support of at least a majority of the military. In the final analysis the army was still the power broker in Mexican politics. Even Obregón, who had a great deal of personal popularity,

could not be assured of continuing in power if a
majority of the generals turned against him.   In
addition, of course, Obregón's assassination in 1928
demonstrated all too conclusively that the arrangement
depended on the continued mortality of the two protago-
nists.   There was no institutionalization.   Such time-
honored practices as rule by the caudillo, continuismo,
caciquismo at the local level, and the army as political
arbiter were all extremely attractive and readily available   options   to   the   Revolutionary   generals   in   the
1920s.[13]
          In   spite   of   the   political   phenomena   described
above,   Mexican   society   was   undergoing   changes   in   the
1920s,   which   had   political   consequences.   Basically,
these changes were "modernizing" in the parlance of the
developmentalists.   Economic   growth,   though   moderate,
was   greater   than   it   had   been   during   the   preceding   violent decade.   Manufacturing increased its share of the
national   product,   and   road   and   rail   transport   both
became increasingly available in Mexico.   At the same
time   rapid   urbanization,   originating   in   the   extensive
rural violence of the previous decade, continued through
the   1920s.   Voter   participation   was   also   increasing
during the period.   In 1917, Carranza had been elected
in an election in which a total of 812,928 votes had
been cast.   The number of voters ascended to 1,181,550
in   1920;   1,593,257   in   1924;   and   1,670,453   in   1928.
During the decade of the 1920's there was a 100 percent
increase   in   voter   participation   in   Mexico.   One   could
hypothesize,   then,   that   the   "crisis   of   participation"
hypothesized by LaPalombara and Weiner was beginning in
Mexico in the 1920s.
          Taking all of the socio-economic and political data
as indices of "modernization," a case can certainly be
made that the development of a major political party at
the end of the 1920s was a "natural" outgrowth of the
changes that had occurred in Mexico.   The major problem
with   the   hypothesis,   aside   from   its   automaticity,   is
that precisely the same changes were occurring in other
Latin   American   societies   during   the   decade,   but   the
relevant political instituions did not emerge in these
other societies.   Many other Latin American countries
were   undergoing   similar   economic,   societal,   and
political   changes.   The   crucial   variable   in   Mexico,
missing in the other countries of Latin America, was the
variable of political leadership, but political leadership of a special kind which has not yet been widely
recognized, either in the literature or in the countries
where this leadership existed.[14]

The Leader

          Plutarco   Elias   Calles   was   a   politician   and   a   survivor. He was also a person who, once he found politics, enjoyed and understood the uses of political power.

However much he enjoyed political power, Calles lacked the charisma exhibited by Obregón (or Yrigoyen and other Latin American leaders of the era) necessary for personal domination of the political process. Where Obregón could command through sheer force of personality and appeal Calles had to resort to less traditional (in the Mexican context) means. Calles, who lacked the stage presence for the masses and bonhomerie for the elite groups, was forced to exert political power through institutions, and where institutions did not exist, he was forced to create them in order to extend his own political power. Thus the crucial ingredient for institution-building in a time of political crisis—a political leader who was forced to exert power through institutions he could control instead of the exertion of individual charisma—was added to the necessary elements of modernization and political crisis which existed in Mexico during the 1920s.

What were the influences in Calles' life that led to the development of his approach to political power? Many of the details of his life are unclear, and most biographies fall into the camp either of hagiography or vitriol, with Calles being viewed as either saint or sinner.[15] Obviously he was neither, but was a politician in an era dominated by the caudillos, ideologues, and warriors, most of whom had disappeared from the scene by 1928.

Although the facts of Calles' birth and early life are sketchy, several facts appear clear. First, he was born into very poor circumstances in Guaymas, Sonora, a part of Mexico far away from the centers of power and wealth. Second, he never referred publicly to his parents or his early life. Whether this was because he preferred to forget what must have been a painful episode or because of his natural taciturnity is not known. The fact remains, however, that in a country where ancestry, even in an age of revolution, was important, Calles preferred to forget his past. Growing up poor and unsure of one's antecedents in the dusty streets of Guaymas or Hermosillo probably produced a strong sense of the present and the pragmatic in the young boy. The early years, the poverty, the lack of any "place" in society seem to have produced in Calles a fierce determination to succeed. Success and power were to be the guiding stars of Calles' life. They were in fact the only true ideology (aside from his virulent anti-Catholicism) that Calles ever had. He was a pragmatist first, last, and always, even in an age of ideologues.[16]

Calles spent most of his early life in and around Guaymas, working variously as assistant teacher, school inspector, newspaper reporter, and farmer. He was not conspicuously successful at any occupation. Accounts of his school teaching vary from glowing reports which indicate that he was firm but fair, to reports that he showed up drunk most of the time, and was fired from his job. All but the most adulatory biographers state that Calles also engaged in other activities to make ends meet. He was, at various times, a seller of contraband goods imported from the United States, a bartender, and the owner of a whorehouse in Agua Prieta on the U.S. border. During this early phase of his life, however, Calles exhibited an interest in politics. Although apparently not a member, he showed great sympathy for the Club Verde in Guaymas, a club of young dissidents combating the continued control over Sonoran politics by a triumvirate of Ramon Corral, Raphael Irrazabal, and General Luis G. Torres; all of whom were stooges of the dictator Porfirio Diaz. Calles also subscribed to the newspaper "Regeneration," an opposition newspaper published in Los Angeles but distributed rather widely throughout Sonora.

In spite of this interest in politics, however, it appears that if it had not been for the outbreak of the Mexican Revolution of 1910, Calles' life might have continued in an unexceptional way. Although he was an early supporter of Francisco Madero and the ideals of The Revolution, Calles did not really enter into the fray until after Madero's assassination in February, 1913. Immediately after the event, Calles offered his services to the Revolutionary forces then organizing in Sonora under the leadership of Alvaro Obregón. For the next five years Calles' life (as was that of most Mexicans) was consumed by revolutionary battles. Calles was not, as some biographers make him out to be, a conspicuous success as a military man. Nevertheless, that quality of organization and survival which characterized so much of his life seems to best describe Calles' military career. The career centered around the town of Naco, in Sonora, defended by forces loyal to the Huerta government. Calles initially failed miserably in an attempt to take the town, but if not a hero, Calles was an organizer. After the initial defeat, he had the sense to secure as his second-in-command Colonel Arnulfo Gonzales, who was a good military strategist, and who subsequently fought most of Calles' battles while Calles did the organizational work. The result of all this was Calles' finest hour as a soldier--the second battle of Naco--in which his troops, now occupying the town, successfully defended it against Huerta's troops.

Probably the most important result of this phase of Calles' life was his friendship with Alvaro Obregón; for Obregón (who was a charismatic military genius) rapidly became one of the major Revolutionary leaders in Mexico, and the undisputed leader in Sonora. Fighting alter-

nately against the Huertistas and against fellow revolutionary Pancho Villa, Obregón soon gained a position of
power in Revolutionary circles surpassed only by
Venustiano Carranza. And Calles moved with Obregón:

> Calles was not a military man. For him the
> military career was not an end in itself, but
> merely the means of having in his grasp the
> power necessary to develop his vast political
> platform.[17]

Calles' political career began once the constitu-
tionalists, led by Venustiano Carranza and Alvaro
Obregón, had consolidated their power. Carranza named
Calles first as chief of the Military Zone of the Northwest and later as Secretary of Industry and Commerce in
his first cabinet in 1917. In 1919, when it became
apparent that Carranza would impose his own candidate
for the presidential elections scheduled for the next
year, the Sonoran triumvirate, composed of Obregón,
Calles, and Adolfo de la Huerta, went into opposition.
The Sonorans' rebellion against Carranza was the last
successful rebellion in Mexico, and the result was that
Alvaro Obregon was elected President in 1920. Carranza
was assassinated while trying to escape Mexico City with
a great deal of booty.

Under Obregón's presidency Calles' political star
rose even higher. First as Minister of War and Navy and
later as Minister of Gobernacion, Calles played a
leading role in the politics of those years.[18]
During his stint as Minister of War and Navy, Calles
began the de-politicization of the military--a process
that was completed only in the 1940s.

Calles was, of course, the official candidate for
the presidency in 1924, which marked a schism in the
Sonoran triumvirate. This time, Adolfo de la Huerta was
the "bastard" candidate for the president, and once
again the election was decided beforehand by force of
arms. Calles and Obregón prevailed, and in 1924 Calles
was inaugurated as President of Mexico.

Calles' presidency (1924-1928) is the subject of a
great deal of controversy for two major reasons. First,
it is apparent that Calles went a long way toward pro-
voking the cristero rebellion which broke out during the
period.[19] Second, Calles has been accused of
entreguismo with the United States and its Ambassador to
Mexico, Dwight Morrow.[20] Although no definitive
reading is possible, it appears that Calles was
determined to break the power of the Catholic Church in
Mexico once and for all, and accepted (even relished)
the necessity of an open confrontation as the means of
accomplishing his goal. Probably Calles' virulent anti-
Catholicism played a role in his decision to provoke the
Church to open conflict. The fact is, however, that by

the end of the rebellion in 1929, the power of the Church in Mexican politics had been virtually eliminated. The subject of entreguismo has been dealt with in an equally polemical manner. Probably the judgment of Rafael Carrillo, then Secretary-General of the Communist Party in Mexico, and certainly no friend of Calles', presents a balanced view of Calles' dealings with Morrow and the United States, especially on the issue of ownership of oil properties:

> First, the cristero rebellion explains the concessions Calles had to make in 1927. His concessions were a result of a set of factors that weakened his government. Calles never forgot who our neighbor to the north is, and knew how to give in when he had to.[21]

Perhaps, the most important aspects of Calles' administration—the beginings of modern Mexico—were overshadowed by the twin controversies over religion and oil. Although the following comments are not shared by everyone, they do appear to represent two balanced accounts of the Calles presidency. Jesus Silva Herzog is a noted Mexican historian, whereas Barry Carr is an English scholar interested in the growth of the labor movement during the period, but both come to the same conclusion. First Herzog:

> Calles was revealed as a great statesman, one of the greatest in Mexico. Let's remember what this man did for the country while he was president, as he brought about great reforms rapidly. First, in 1925 he established the Bank of Mexico. Second, he established for the first time what we call here the tax on income. Third, he organized the national roads commission, and built the first highway between Mexico and the city of Puebla. In the fourth place, he organized the National Irrigation Commission, which is now the Secretariat of Water Resources. In the fifth place, we should refer to the Agrarian Reform. Calles thought of agrarian reform in an integral manner, establishing the National Bank of Agricultural Credit on March, 1926, and placing an agricultural school near each branch of the Bank.[22]

Carr seconds Herzog's judgment:

> Calles' presidency marked a decisive break with the past in several respects. From more than a decade of armed struggle, Mexico had emerged with few of the requirements for rapid economic

development. In the four years after 1924 a start was made in providing a modern infrastructure: striking progress was achieved in communications, roads, rail, and telephones. His solution for specific problems and his vision of a new Mexico took on a semicorporatist character, a tendency particularly clear in his attitude toward the technical backwardness of Mexican industry.[23]

Throughout all the commentaries--pro and con--on Calles' presidency, two things stand out. First, Calles took action; to weaken some institutions and to strengthen others, but most importantly to strengthen the power of the central government. Second, Calles was creating the institutions necessary for the emergence of a modern Mexico and not surprisingly, the extension of his own political power. Once again, only someone who understood and enjoyed the uses of political power could have simultaneously fought the cristero rebellion, come to an agreement with an outraged and powerful neighbor to the north, and created a set of modern institutions out of near anarchy in a period of four years.

Alvaro Obregón, the great caudillo, was of course the "official" presidential candidate in 1928, but this time two "bastard" candidates came forward. General Francisco Serrano and General Arnulfo Gomes both attacked the reelection of Obregón and, when it became apparent that the election would not be fair, they took to the battlefield, only to be defeated by the Calles-Obregon forces. Thus far, every post-Revolution election had first been disputed on the battlefield and, only when the military verdict was in, was the political verdict delivered.

Obregón's victory was, however, short-lived. On the afternoon of July 18, 1928, while attending a dinner in his honor, Obregón was shot to death by a religious mystic. Although it is apparent that Calles had little to gain by sponsoring such an act and that he and Obregón were good friends, suspicion began to center on Calles. Calles immediately acted to defuse these suspicions by removing his chief of police (who was an anti-Obregonista) and by appointing Obregón partisans to the commission investigating the assassination. Once again, decisive action worked, as it soon became apparent that the assassin was a member of an extremist Catholic group opposed by both Calles and Obregón.

Once the immediate crisis was passed, however, Calles was faced with a major decision. He was now the sole remaining caudillo from the Revolution of 1910. All the others--Madero, Zapata, Villa, Carranza, de la Huerta, and now Obregón--had been killed. Should he, in the time-honored tradition of caudillos everywhere, seize the reins of power and assume a new dictatorship?

The very existence of the tradition argued in favor of
such a course. On the other hand the shorter but
equally potent tradition of the Revolution prohibited a
president from succeeding himself. The political
realities facing Calles were mixed. On one hand he was
still suspect by the Obregonistas who, even with their
leader dead, still constituted a strong political force.
On the other hand, Calles had courted organized labor in
the person of Luis Morones and could count on the
support of Morones and his followers. Certainly Calles'
chances of continuing in power were quite good, even
though such an attempt would undoubtedly precipitate a
power struggle and possibly even another armed revolt.

Some time between July 18 and September 1, which
was the date for the annual State of the Union address
to Congress, Calles made a decision not to try to continue in office. Instead, as he stated in his speech on
September 1, he would call for an end to caudillismo and
create a new era of political institutions instead of
personalities. Specifically, Calles called for the
creation of a new political party, federal in character,
but a party that would bring together for the first time
all the different ideological and personal currents
which had sprung from the Revolution. Once again, as is
the case with most of his political decisions, Calles'
ultimate motives went with him to the grave, and
scholars have been left to speculate as to why he chose
the solution to the political crisis. Many authors
ascribe purely base motives for the decision:

> President Calles was faced with a dilemma. His
> term in office had expired, and not even
> Obregón had attempted to impose himself for a
> second term immediately. The only solution
> seemed to be a resort to continuismo--to
> impose a weaker politician in the presidency
> while Calles himself remained the power behind
> the throne.[24]

> Calles emerged the full-fledged caudillo he had
> said Mexico would be well rid of. He became,
> in short, the modern political machine boss so
> familiar in American politics.[25]

Other authors take a more balanced view:

> He...used the moment of tension and strife to
> attempt a bridge between the tradition of the
> caudillo and political democracy. The moment
> was tense with implicit tragedy, for the logic
> of political tradition required either a
> tyranny or a convulsion. That neither came to
> pass is to the credit of Calles, and it must be
> recognized as the beginning of that change in

the political atmosphere which has since brought relative peace to the country.[26]

Ricardo Zevada, one of Calles' most assiduous bio-graphers, has tried to re-create Calles' mental process during this period.

President Calles - reviews what had been the history of Mexico in the last fifteen years, from the uprising of The Citadel of 18 February 1913, to the moment in which the president-elect falls in La Bombilla, the 17th of July, 1928.

A conclusion...could be that in all that epoch ...political power was gained or lost by force of arms, by the violent confrontation of armed citizens, by regular or improvised armies, generals and officers who placed their personal ambition almost always above the general interest.

The leaders of all the movements wanted power, some got it, others didn't, because they were defeated, and those who had it transmitted it to their own men. All the debate revolved around personalities. Disunion was the rule, confirmed by the conduct of the caudillos, and they disputed among themselves more their merits for taking over the government than their abilities to comply with the promises of the Revolution.

President Calles knew well, at the end of his term, that if things continued this way, it would not be possible to achieve stability of leadership, so necessary to guarantee con-tinuity of revolutionary action.[27]

Once again, the judgment of Jesus Silva Herzog probably comes closest to the truth. After stating that, in his opinion, the most important political fact for Mexico today was the creation of the PNR in 1929 (which was the work of Calles), Herzog goes on to say:

It seems to me possible that General Calles thought about that (maintaining control over the Revolution) but it seems to me even more possible that he thought not only of that but also of the institutionalization of the country. So that Calles' enemies may say that he was motivated by nothing more than his ambition, but Calles was not only an ambitious person, he was a man with good endowments as a

statesman and with an authentic patriotism. I
believe that you have to think that if there
were certain personal motives there were also
those of a national character and of searching
for the good of the nation.[28]

The important point is that at this critical juncture Calles pragmatically decided to create a political
party instead of continuing down the familiar road of
open caudillismo. The PNR came into being during the
first National Convention of the Party held in Queretaro
in March, 1929.[29] In the interim Calles, who had
been named chairman of the Organizing Committee, had
resigned his post, ostensibly in order that he would not
dominate the Convention. A reading of the proceedings
indicates that in fact it was Calles' show all the way,
from the selection of a presidential candidate to the
creation of the Party statutes. The candidate of the
Obregonistas, Aaron Saenz, withdrew from the balloting
and left the nomination to Pascual Ortiz Rubio, Calles'
candidate. The Party statutes, which were also the work
of Calles, created an organization quite similar to that
of the modern-day PRI. The Central Executive Committee
(CEN) which today controls the Party was the major
creation of the 1929 Convention, as it lay the groundwork for the centralization of power at the national
level of the Party. Interestingly, Calles made no
speeches at the Convention until near the end when yet
another army rebellion broke out. At this point Calles
made the dramatic announcement that he was leaving to
head the fight against the rebels, and would assume the
post of Secretary of War. The rebellion, which was the
last by the army in Mexican history, was crushed within
a few weeks.

Conclusion

Mexico entered a new era in her history after 1929;
one of institutions rather than caudillos. Personalities are still important in Mexican politics, but one
is impressed with the corporatist nature not only of
Mexican politics but of Mexican society itself.[30]
Whether this is good or bad in the context of Mexico
today is up to the individual, but certainly Mexican
society began to change dramatically during the nine
months from July, 1928, to April, 1929. After having
reviewed the events and personalities of the time and
the theories as to the reasons for the changes, a main
conclusion of the Chapter must be that societal and
economic changes, while necessary conditions for
political changes and the creation of political parties
are not, in themselves, sufficient conditions for such
events. As the story of the creation of the PNR demon-

strates, societal and economic changes must be accompanied by political leadership to take advantage of those changes. Calles had a political choice in 1928, and he chose a course of action that led to the creation of a political party. He might well have chosen otherwise. We might well label Calles a "politician" or, in Daniel James' terms, a "political boss." For James, who may be correct in his assessment of Calles, neglects the all-important difference between political bosses (who control political machines) and the romantic caudillos, most of whom operated on a strictly personalist basis. The difference, of course, is that the politician creates a machinery that may outlast the political boss himself. This is, of course, what happened in Mexico as Calles later made the fatal political mistake of assuming that he could continue to control Mexican politics utilizing the political talents of Lázaro Cárdenas. Calles' mistake (perhaps the only one of his political career) was two-fold: he underestimated the political talents of Cárdenas, and he also overestimated his own control of the party bureaucracy.[31] Perhaps this final mistake becomes more understandable when taken in the context of Calles' personal misfortunes, which include the death of his second, much younger, wife and his own continued severe health problems, which became worse with age.[32] Whatever the cause of Calles' final demise as a political leader, his early institutionalizing work had already been accomplished, and the crucial role of political leadership in an atmosphere of social change had been fulfilled.

An understanding of the type of personality needed to play the role of political leadership is as important as an understanding of the societal conditions required for the development of political parties. A strong case can be made that a pragmatic Calles, rather than a Madero or an Obregón is the type of political leader necessary for the creation of political institutions. Calles provides evidence that the political leadership of the pragmatic, non-ideological type is a crucial element in the development of enduring political institutions, and that the charismatic leader has severe shortcomings in this process. The charismatic leader generally has no need of institutions. Obregón could govern without party machinery and, in fact, such machinery would be useless to him. Calles, on the other hand, needed institutions (which he could manipulate) in order to exert power. Perhaps the rather sneering observation by Vicente Lombardo Toledano that "Calles had no ideology" was the greatest compliment paid him, as well as a prescient comment on Mexican politics.[33]

The final possible observation involves commentary on current Mexican politics and prospects for institutional developments either within or outside the PRI similar to those which occurred in the late 1920s. A

combination of factors which include the increasingly
complex nature of Mexican society, rapid urbanization,
economic growth, plus the Reforma Politica instituted by
the Mexican government in 1978, has led several observers to suggest that political developments leading
to greater party competition in Mexico may be in the
offing, and recent municipal elections in that country
tend to confirm this. Specifically, Jose Luis Reyna has
suggested that societal changes coupled with economic
growth will produce increased and varied political
demands which will culminate in the re-structuring of
Mexican politics along multi-party lines. Once again,
of course, we are presented with the almost automatic
"middle sectors" thesis: the emergence of varied
interest groups as a result of societal changes will
result ultimately in the creation of new and varied
political institutions. If this study has any significance, it is to suggest that the political changes do
not occur automatically, and that until and unless
Mexico's newly-emerging interest groups find the type of
political leadership which was vital to the changes in
the 1920s, these changes will not take place, and the
incongruence between Mexico's social and economic
institutions and its political institutions will grow
ever greater. Once before, when the incongruence
between society and politics was great, Mexican
political leadership seized the moment and brought about
necessary political change. Perhaps, now that Mexico is
once again faced with a growing incongruence and social
conditions are "ripe" for the political changes, her
political leadership will be equal to the task. It
will, however, be the vital element of political leadership, and not merely anonymous social forces, which will
ultimately bring about these changes in the Mexican
political system.

Notes

1. The PRI has undergone two name changes since its inception. It was founded in 1929 as the Partido Nacional Revolucionario (PNR). In 1938 its name was changed to the Partido de la Revolucion Mexicana (PRM). Finally, in 1946, the party became the Partido Revolucionario Institucional (PRI).

2. Jose Luis Reyna, "Movilizacion y Participacion Politica," in Perfil de Mexico en 1980, (Mexico: Universidad Nacional Autonoma de Mexico, 1976), pp. 519-520.

3. Joseph LaPalombara and Myron Weiner (eds.), Political Parties and Political Development (Princeton: Princeton University Press, 1966).

4. Ibid., p. 21.

5. Walt W. Rostow, in his book The Stages of Economic Growth, estimates that Argentina entered a period of sustained economic growth during the 1920s.

6. We use here the concept of institutionalization developed by Samuel P. Huntington in his book, Political Order in Developing Societies. An excellent study of the institutionalizaton of the PRI is the unpublished manuscript by Maria Antonieta Benejam, "Partido Revolucionario Institucional, Proceso de Institucionalizacion de un Partido Politico," unpublished thesis for Licenciatura en Sociologia, Facultad de ciencias Politicas y Sociales, Universidad Nacional Autonoma de Mexico, 1972.

7. Edwin Lieuwen, Mexican Militarism: The Political Rise and Fall of the Revolutionary Army (Albuquerque: University of New Mexico Press, 1968). For an excellent and authoritative account of Calles' attempt to professionalize the army, see Jean Meyer, et. al., Historia de la Revolucion Mexicana (Mexico: El Colegio de Mexico, 1977), Vol. II, "Estado y Sociedad con Calles," pp. 60-76.

8. There are several excellent books and manuscripts on this period of Mexican history. The Meyer book listed above, Roger D. Hansen, La Politica del Desarrollo Mexicano (Mexico: Siglo XXI Editores, 1967), and an unpublished manuscript, Maria Antonia Benejam Dominquez, "Partido Revolucionario Institucional, Processo de Institucionalizacion de un Partido Politico," all give excellent accounts of the period from 1917 to 1929.

9. Benejam, p. 54.

10. Meyer, p. 97.

11. Robert Scott, Mexican Government in Transition (Urbana: University of Illinois Press, 1964), p. 119.

12. All of the evidence for this understanding is circumstantial, but most authors writing on the period come to the conclusion that this alternation of power was the aim of the two Sonorans.

46

13. Pablo Gonzalez Casanova, Democracy in Mexico (New York: Oxford University Press, 1970), p. 199.
14. One finds in Mexico, for example, a strong yearning for the charismatic politician and a strong distaste for the institution builders. Calles is not considered a member of the revolutionary "family."
15. There are numerous biographies of Calles, all of which were utilized in the preparation of this work. These works include: Francis McCullagh, Red Mexico (New York: Wadsworth, 1929); Holland D. Watkins, "Plutarco Calles," (unpublished Ph.D. Dissertation, Texas Technological University, 1968); Fernando Medina, Calles: Un Destino Melancolico (Mexico: Editorial Juz, 1960); Roman Puente, Hombres de la Revolucion: Calles (Los Angeles: n.p., 1933); Gustavo Casasola, Biografia Illustrada de General Plutarco Elias Calles (Mexico: n.p., 1975); Juan de Dios Bojorquez, Plutarco Elias Calles, Rasgos Biográficos (Mexico: PRI, Comision Editorial, 1976); Ricardo J. Zevada, Calles el Presidente (Mexico: Editorial Nuestro Tiempo, 1977); Amado Chaverri Matamoros El Verdadero Calles (Mexico: Editorial Patria, 1933); Luciano Kubli, "Calles, El Hombre y su Gobierno," unpublished typescript in Archivo General de la Nacion, Mexico; and Carlos Peyrera, Mexico Falsificado: Tomo II (Mexico: Editorial Polis, 1949). Additional biographical material may be found in the following works: Jean Meyer, op. cit., Roberto Blanco Moheno, Cronica de la Revolucion Mexican, Tomo III, Vasconcelos, Calles, Cardenas (Mexico: Libro Mex, 1961); Julio Cuadros Caldas, El Comunismo Criolla (Puebla, Mexico: n.p., 1930); A. Gil Pihaloup, El General Calles y el Sindicalismo (Mexico: Herrero Hnos y Sucesores, 1925); Emilio Portes Gil, Quince Años de la Politica Mexicana (Mexico: Ediciones Botas de Mexico, 1941); Juan Gualberta Amaya, Los Gobiernos de Obregon, Calles, y Regimenes Peleles Derivados del Callismo (Mexico: published by author, 1947); Alberto Brenauntz, Material Historico de Obregón a Calles (Mexico: Avelar Hnos. Impresores, 1973); and Calles' Presidential papers held in the Presidential branch of the Archivo General de la Nacion.
16. All of Calles' biographers comment on his lack of ideology and his pragmatism. An examination of his Presidential papers reveals an extremely pragmatic approach to life and politics.
17. Kubli, op. cit., p. 20.
18. Calles' presidential papers are mixed with Obregón's. It became apparent while reading the papers that Obregón relied greatly on Calles as the organizer during his presidency.
19. See Viva Christo Rey! by David C. Bailey (Austin, University of Texas Press, 1974) for the best account in English of the Cristero rebellion.
20. The two became good friends, although Calles

47

remained a firm nationalist to the end.

21. Interview with Rafael Carrillo, former Secretary-General of the Communist Party of Mexico.

22. Jesus Silva Herzog, as quoted in James W. Wilkie and Edna Monzon de Wilkie, Mexico Visto en el Siglo XX (Mexico: Instituto Mexicano de Investigaciones Economicas, 1969), p. 637.

23. Barry Carr, Organized Labour and the Mexican Revolution: 1915-1928 (Latin American Centre, St. Anthony's College, Oxford University, Occasional Papers, 1972), p. 20.

24. Scott, p. 121.

25. Daniel James, Mexico and the Americans (New York: MacMillian, 1963), p. 246.

26. Frank Tannenbaum, Mexico, The Struggle for Peace and Bread (New York: A. A. Knopf, 1951), p. 67.

27. A. Zevada, pp. 71-73.

28. Herzog, as quoted in Wilkie, p. 658.

29. Proceedings of the Convention are contained in La Democracia Social en Mexico (Mexico: Partido Nacional Revolucionario, 1929).

30. This is a personal impression based upon experiences during a ten-month existence in Mexico.

31. By the time of the second convention of the PNR in December, 1973, the Party's Central Committee had changed membership completely. While all the members of the original CEN were Calles' men, it is impossible to identify the 1933 group as Callistas. For listings of the two groups, see Memoria de la Segunda Convencion Nacional del PNR (Mexico: PNR, 1934), pp. 14-51. Also interesting is the fact that at the first Convention there were innumerable "Vivas" for Calles, while at the second Convention the only "Viva" recorded in the official proceedings was for Cardenas (p. 57).

32. Calles' presidential papers reveal several trips to the United States (Los Angeles, San Francisco, the Mayo Clinic, New York) for treatment and operations for what had been diagnosed as severe angina. This condition grew progressively worse as Calles grew older. Calles' first wife died in Los Angeles on June 2, 1927. His second wife died in 1931.

33. Wilkie, p. 273.

3
Rafael Trujillo
and the Dominican Party

Few political leaders in the twentieth century have
been as sanguinary, venal, and corrupt as Generalissimo
Rafael Leonidas Trujillo y Molina in the Dominican
Republic. From the day he assumed power in that unhappy
little country in 1930, until his death by assassination
in 1961, Trujillo ruled "his" country with an iron hand.
Few dictators in the period ruled so completely as did
Trujillo, and few amassed the personal fortune from
their rule as did the Generalissimo. Trujillo had many
different facets of his rule, but one of the major
organizations he created to further his control was a
political party--the Dominican Party (Partido Dominicano
--PD). In what is perhaps the greatest irony of
Dominican politics, and one of the great ironies of
Latin American politics, the PD, which was created by
Trujillo solely to further his own personal ambition,
and which was disbanded shortly after the hated dictator was assassinated, has since reappeared, under a
new name, as a major balance wheel in the largely democratic politics of the post-Trujillo years. Or rather,
we should say the machinery of the PD has persisted into
the new era; the party as it was originally constituted
did disappear in 1961.[1] However, Joaquin Balaguer,
who had been one of Trujillo's minor lackeys, reappeared
on the Dominican political scene during the U.S.-
supervised 1966 elections with an ostensibly new
political party--the Partido Reformista (Reformist Party
--PR)--which had as its basis the old political organizations established by Trujillo and his PD in every
village in the Dominican Republic.[2] Balaguer and his
"new" political organization proceeded to win not only
the 1966 election (which was, perhaps, the fairest in
the history of the Dominican Republic) but also the
elections of 1970 and 1974. Although the PR and
Balaguer lost in 1978 and again in 1982, it has remained
a major political force in the nation's politics.[3]

48

The Environment

The Dominican Party was officially founded on March 11, 1932, with Rafael Leonidas Trujillo listed as its Director. Plans for the Party had been underway, however, almost from the time Trujillo assumed power in the Dominican Republic in August, 1930.[4] In a sense, by 1932 Trujillo <u>was</u> the environment in the Dominican Republic, as he dominated not only the political structure but the entire life of the nation. Trujillo was no ordinary dictator, and the PD was organized by him as yet one more link in his total control of the nation.

In spite of Trujillo's domination of Dominican national life, there were, of course other forces at work in the nation, especially during the early years of the regime. Foremost among these were the intervention of the United States (1915 to 1924), the decline into disorder and disintegration of the government of Horacio Vasquez (1924-1930), and the anterior dictatorship of Ulises Heureaux, from 1882 to 1899.

The United States' intervention in and occupation of the Dominican Republic occurred against the well-known backdrop of the imperialist urge in the United States, which had come to the foreground at the turn of the century, and the Roosevelt Corollary, which gave some shred of legal and political sanction to that urge. This was not, however, the first time the U.S. had looked southward to the Caribbean. As early as 1866, immediately after the U.S. Civil War, Presidents and Secretaries of State began various machinations aimed at either territorial concessions which would permit a U.S. naval base at Camana Bay or, as later developed, outright annexation of the Dominican Republic. That nothing came of these intentions was due more to internal U.S. politics than to any slackening of U.S. influence in the Dominican Republic.[5]

By the early twentieth century, however, internal circumstances in the U.S. had changed. Most of the political, moral, and social opposition to U.S. intervention abroad had been swept away by the euphoria of the Spanish-American war, and the "right" and "duty" of the United States to regulate the conduct of others had been converted into what amounted to a holy national cause in the eyes of the public. To Presidents like Teddy Roosevelt and his successors, intervention also appeared to serve the national interest by keeping European powers out of what was now regarded as an American lake. The key, as far as the Dominican Republic was concerned, was the extraordinary political instability occasioned by the assassination, in 1899, of the dictator Heureaux. Steps were taken, beginning in 1905, to secure U.S. interests in the nation. From that time on, the eventual result—full U.S. occupation of the country from 1915 to 1924—was inevitable.[6]

The American occupation of the Dominican Republic was marked, as were all American occupations--by an extraordinary lack of knowledge of the country being occupied. Few of the officers and almost none of the enlisted personnel could speak Spanish, and few made any attempt to understand the history and folkways of the society in which they were involved. One result was a certain number of atrocities committed by American military against Dominicans. The resulting counter-terror produced in the Americans a recognition of the necessity for some kind of local constabulary to support their rule. Accordingly, in 1917, the Dominican National Guard was established. On January 11, 1919, Rafael Trujillo received his commission as one of 16 new Second Lieutenants in the Guard. By May, 1928, Trujillo had risen to the rank of Brigadier General and Chief of the National Army. He had found his path to power, thanks to the Americans who provided his first step.[7]

With the departure of the Marines and the election of President Horacio Vasquez in 1924, the Dominican Republic emerged from total American domination, and entered a relatively short period of open politics. Fortunately for Trujillo, Vasquez, although honest and a good politician, was beginning to age and lose some of his political skills. Bickering broke out within Vasquez's rather personalist political party over the succession, with no one commanding the broad popular support enjoyed by Vasquez. The two major rivals for power vied for Trujillo's support, and this further enhanced the General's position. Finally, in 1930, after waiting in vain for Vasquez to die, Trujillo moved to gain ultimate power. In a series of moves beginning in February and ending with his installation in the Presidency in August, Trujillo established himself as the unquestioned ruler of the Dominican Republic. The old institutions which had been precariously established in the six years since the end of the American occupa-tion disappeared almost overnight, as did the former political actors. Some were killed, some were exiled, and only ex-President Vasquez eventually returned to the Dominican Republic, to die an embittered old man in 1936. Trujillo had triumphed over the weak institutions and ineffectual leaders who had tried to bring democracy to the Dominican Republic during their short time in power. He had also triumphed over the United States, which could never decide whether Trujillo should be supported or condemned, and therefore stood by and did nothing.

The Dominican Republic, like other Latin American nations which suffered under twentieth century tyrants, had its nineteenth century tyrants as well. The reign of Ulises (Lilis) Heureaux (1882-1899) introduced many aspects of what we would, today, call totalitarian rule to the Dominican Republic. Heureaux was, in many aspects a model for Trujillo in his complete control over the institutions of the country, and in his accent on building public projects.[8] "Unlike his predecessors, he left the country richer in industries, agriculture, and communications--and his friends and relatives richer in the process."[9] After discussing many other remarkable similarities between Heureaux and his twentieth century successor, Selden Rodman concludes:

> Only in respect to the techniques of the modern totalitarian state--the single party, the mass rallies, the propaganda mills, the rewriting of history, the indoctrination of children--did Ulises Heureaux yield anything in refinements of despotism to his infamous successor.[10]

We might add that Heureaux's end, by assassination, was also the fate of Trujillo.

The point is that Trujillo had a model, and that model was Ulises Heureaux. The model was, unlike some other models that might have been followed, that of a dictator who maintained power through cunning, hard work, and manipulation of the various sectors of society, rather than through direct appeals to the masses. In this sense, although both Heureaux and Trujillo employed many totalitarian techniques, they eschewed one that has become identified with many twentieth century totalitarians--the speech from the balcony. If Heureaux (who was an imposing figure) was no demagogue, neither was Trujillo. He had a high-pitched, almost squeaky voice and was never able to sway the masses of the people with rhetoric. Unlike Juan Peron in Argentina, or Peron's hero in Germany, Trujillo had to rely on the bureaucratic approach to dictatorship in order to succeed--and he had Heureaux as his model.

In a real sense, Heureaux, the American intervention, and the years under Vasquez all had a larger meaning for Dominican politics before Trujillo, and the type of social and political environment into which Trujillo emerged. Dominican society had, by 1931, become debased by over a century of political chaos, bloody dictatorships, and thralldom to a potent, racially and socially different, power to the north. By the time Trujillo seized power, the societal restraints against such an occurrence (and the subsequent bloody horrors of the Trujillo years) had all but disappeared in that unhappy country. Although it was written after the Trujillo regime, La Comunidad Mulata, by Pedro Andres Perez Cabral, describes the progressive deterioration of Dominican society:

> In the Dominican Republic, the frequent occurrence of the despotic system--a common

occurrence in Hispanic America--represented by
four caudillista regimes that have been progressively undermining the structure of the
precarious society, have culminated disas-
trously in the total disintegration of ethical
principles and social norms that, for obvious
reasons and inherent in the Hispanic-American
formation in general and the Dominican in
particular, never achieved the solidity and
firmness of other societies generated in
distinct historic and geographic conditions.[11]

Perez, an anthropologist, makes a case that the
basic problem in the Dominican Republic stems from the
character of its society. Others argue that the society
has been formed by historical occurrences, both before
and after independence. The outstanding fact is,
however, that of approximately one hundred years of
independence before Trujillo, eighty of those years had
been spent under one of three dictatorships, or American
occupation. Small wonder that Trujillo was able to
seize power as easily as he did, and smaller wonder that
he was able to impose his will for as long and as completely as he did. Where, in many other Latin American
nations, a modicum of institutional development had
occurred, in the Dominican Republic there was none, and
consequently no resistance to ultimate tyranny.

The Leader

Rafael Trujillo was born in 1891 in the little town
of San Cristobal, eighteen miles west, along the
Caribbean coast, from Santo Domingo.[12] Trujillo's
father, Jose Trujillo Valdez, had been born in Bani in
1864, the illegitimate son of Jose Trujillo Monagas and
Silveria Valdez. While Trujillo Valdez was in his
infancy, his father returned first to Cuba and later to
Spain, while Silveria engaged in the twin occupations of
raising her son and of participating in the intrigues
and violence that helped maintain "Lilis" Heureaux in
power. Quite probably, the fact that Heureaux was a
negro attracted Trujillo's paternal grandmother to his
cause. She was a mulatto, a fact that forever afterward
affected Trujillo's life. On his maternal side,
moreover, Trujillo's grandmother was the illegitimate
daughter of a Haitian army officer and a Haitian woman,
and was the source of the Haitian strain in Trujillo.
Trujillo's mother, Altagracia Julia Molina, was the
daughter of this pair.
Jose Trujillo Valdez and Altagracia Julia Molina
were married in San Cristobal on September 29, 1887.
Trujillo Valdez was a small businessman in San

Cristobal; pleasant, amiable, but licentious to an amazing degree, which seems to be the only trait he passed on to his son. Rafael was the third of what eventually came to be eleven brothers and sisters. The Trujillo family was in the context of San Cristobal, upper-middle-class. Crassweller states that "If a social anthropologist of the day had drawn a scale... from the top of the village structure to the bottom,... the Trujillo family would have had to be placed in the seventy-fifth percentile."[13] So the burning sense of lower-class origins and negritude that later scarred Trujillo's personality did not come from his early days in San Cristobal. In fact, his early childhood was rather uneventful, "...a long season of indolence and play in the dusty streets and shaded years, in the company of wandering animals and almost naked playmates."[14] In fact, Trujillo's life was remarkably unremarkable, up until his enlistment in the National Guard in 1919, and his subsequent cooperation with the U.S. Marines and then his meteoric rise to power after 1924. By adolescence, several of the character traits that were to become more marked in later life had, however, already appeared. Rafael was extremely fastidious, already given to the use of perfume, and his extreme interest in women was already apparent. From approximately 1910, when he was nineteen, until 1916, little is known of Trujillo's activities. Much of the record has been deliberately removed, while other parts were never recorded, obviously because Trujillo was at the time just another young man in the rural areas of the Dominican Republic. The future dictator held several jobs; as a telegraph operator, and as assistant in the local post office. He was also married, in 1913 to one Anita Ledesma, who bore him a child. The daughter died a year later, and the marriage was eventually terminated. In 1916, at the age of 25, Trujillo entered into the last stage of his pre-army career, working on a sugar cane plantation in a variety of jobs, mainly as a sort of private policeman, or guarda campestre, in general charge of keeping order on the plantation.

Finally, however, Trujillo found his metier--the army. Just as Plutarco Calles had found himself within the armed chaos of the Mexican revolution, and had risen to the heights, so now Trujillo found himself in an atmosphere congenial to his predilections.

> He had found his role. The life of the army
> was perfectly suited to him in almost all its
> aspects. His knowledge of history was exceed-
> ingly limited, but it was sufficient to inform
> him that the army was the traditional road to
> power and glory in Spanish-American nations,
> and if history had failed him in this, his

instinct would have sufficed. The Army, moreover, was the road to well-being and possibly
to wealth, for in his society the possession of
power had never implied any reluctance to use
it for collateral purposes. The Army, too,
embodied order and discipline and system, and
for all those he had genius, valuing them even
beyond their very considerable merits. Even
the lighter aspects of Army life were congenial
to his temperament. The splendid uniforms, the
parades, the music, the martial pomp, all
nourished his feeling for drama and display.
And the Army, more than any other body in the
inadequate public life of his era, implied
action and achievement and provided an outlet
to his urge to build, to transform, to glorify.[15]

Trujillo's own pronouncements are full of praise
for the military and its virtues. An early sampling
reads:

The National Army, jealous guardian of institutions, to the glory of whose arms I have constituted the better part of my life, the
enthusiasms of my youth and the ardent beating
of my soldier's heart, deserves my most
affectionate dedication, and I must direct all
my efforts, toward its increase, discipline,
brilliance, and respectability, linked to the
sincere desire that the citizenry have the
conviction that Liberty, when there is a pure
soul and a clear concept of duty, is a spotless
virgin who can exist together with the naked
force of the sword without being victimized by
the brutalities of Force.[16]

Most of the words are, of course, window dressing.
Trujillo was a master of the hypocritical phrase, and
also a master of self-deception. The emphasizing of
discipline, duty, and guardianship were, however, themes
that were repeated endlessly in Trujillo's public
remarks over the next thirty-one years. The military
became his life, and all biographers agree that his
military career, first under the United States' occupation and later in the Dominican Army itself, was outstanding. Certain incidents during the period
1918-1930 indicate that Trujillo was, however, already
becoming the master manipulator and schemer who later
emerged in the presidency. This was, of course, a way
to get ahead, and if incompetent superiors could be
unmasked, or if marital dalliances exposed could advance
the young officer's career, so be it. The important
point in assessing Trujillo's political personality,
however, is that he found the discipline, order and

institutionalized aspects of Army life to be utterly congenial. He was, in short, a leader who worked best through institutions which he could manipulate for his own ends.

The 1930 coup which put Trujillo in power for the next thirty-one years has been well-documented else-where. Of course, a major fact that emerges from a study of the coup is the almost complete lack of institutions--institutions that might have impeded Trujillo's seizure of total power. The Army, the only real institution in the country, was dominated by Trujillo. The Catholic Church was one of the more debased churches in Latin America, and suffered from a severe lack of personnel. The only political party worthy of the name was the National Party, under the leadership of President Horacio Vasquez. The problem was, of course, that the party, which had been created at the end of the American occupation in 1924, was completely dependent upon the personal charisma of Vasquez. In fact, the party was almost never called by its real name but was known, instead, as the "Horacistas," after Vasquez's first name. As the President's health failed toward the end of the decade so did the party. By August, 1930, when Trujillo's rolling coup was complete, political parties, such as had existed in the Dominican Republic, had passed into oblivion. The coup had been made much easier by the lack of strong parties that might have opposed it.

Trujillo was, in many ways, the first modern Latin American dictator, presaging to a great extent the modern bureaucratic military dictatorships of the latter half of the twentieth century. In country after country in Latin America during the 1960s and 1970s, the military as an institution had taken over the governance of the society. In almost all the new dictatorships, several themes stand out: a desire for order; an emphasis upon economic growth (not equated with economic justice); the creation of new institutions, especially political parties; and governance by institution rather than by charisma. Trujillo's thirty-one years in power were characterized by the same themes. He was not, in short, a throwback to many of the nineteenth and even twentieth century dictators, such as Juan Vicente Gomez in Venezuela or even Porfirio Diaz in Mexico. These men had governed largely through force of individual personality, and had not bothered to create institutions through which they could manipulate the political process. Trujillo was different. He both believed in and needed institutions to perpetuate his rule, and it soon became obvious that a subservient political party was one of these necessary institutions.

The Party

The Partido Dominicano (Dominican Party - PD) was officially constituted on August 16, 1931, one year after Trujillo had assumed the presidency. Preparations for its establishment had begun almost as soon as Trujillo entered office, as he was aware that (a) the party could serve as a counter-weight to the armed forces and that he could play one institution against the other, and (b) that the existence of a political party would give him the institutional means to extend his control over Dominican society down to the village level. Accordingly the Party, once it was established, soon encompassed almost the entire voting-age population of the Dominican Republic. The Party, of course, had no electoral function to perform. That was decided beforehand by Trujillo, with one or two of his closest advisers. Nevertheless, the Party soon prospered, both in finances and membership. Crassweller points out that in the 1952 elections 1,038,816 votes were cast and the membership roles of the PD contained 1,025,833 names.[17] On one party occasion, Trujillo indicated that everyone who was a loyal citizen was a member of the Party! Only those who remained traitors to the nation were still outside its membership roles.[18] References to the PD are strewn throughout Trujillo's speeches and public declarations.[19] He obviously regarded it as one of his major creations in the Dominican Republic and, although it did not serve the usual functions of a political party in the western democratic sense, nevertheless it was an integral part of Trujillo's control apparatus.

The Party had almost no financial problems. Its expenses were largely financed through a flat ten percent deduction from the paychecks of all its members. Given its immense membership, this produced a great deal of money for Party coffers. Members who were also public officials had their ten percent withheld by the Treasury! Fortified by this tremendous financial boon, the Party went to work. Its major functions somewhat resembled those of old Tammany Hall in New York City. The PD became, in effect, the national welfare agency, dispensing food, medicine, and other forms of largesse to "deserving" party members and other, less fortunate people and institutions. Party offices were soon established in almost every hamlet in the country, and they were always the best-looking buildings in town. Very quickly, Party headquarters became a combination social center and welfare agency in every locality. Almost all public events, whether Party-sponsored or not (most were) were held at the Party headquarters, and it soon became apparent to most Dominicans that good standing with the Party could make life much easier for them and their families.

Trujillo used the PD (as he used everything and
everyone else) to administer his rule. At the first
convention of the Party, in August, 1931, he stated,
"While I occupy the office of chief of state, I shall
govern with the men of the party." As was usual,
Trujillo went on to issue a warning to party members not
to expect too much freedom of decision:

> ...and when, through some quirk of fate, the
> Party no longer is, as I have dreamed of it
> being, the true reflection of the restoring
> work of the government, I will govern with
> those men who have remained faithful to the
> ideal of government that I have tried to place
> at the disposal of all Dominicans.[20]

One of the uses of the PD became apparent as the
"election" of 1934 approached. As was to become the
custom in future "elections" Trujillo went through an
elaborate charade of insisting that he wanted nothing
more than to retire from public office. However, of
course, "the people" would not permit this, so finally
Trujillo accepted what amounted to a draft to run again
for the presidency. The PD's role in this charade (and
subsequent ones as well) was to organize public demon-
stations of support for the Trujillo candidacy and, once
that candidacy was declared, to see to it that a
sufficient number of Dominicans voted in the "election"
(there were no other candidates in 1934--later on,
Trujillo would sometimes produce an "opposition" candidate just to dress things up a bit). The "election" of
1938 demonstrated yet another function of the Party. As
the "election" approached, Trujillo was beset with a
major problem in his relations with the United States,
which had been quite good in the early years of the
regime. On October 2 and 3, 1937, between 10,000 and
20,000 Haitians had been massacred in the Dominican
Republic by Trujillo's apparatus, in response to the
failure of a plot by Trujillo to overthrow the Haitian
government. When word of the massacre finally seeped
out, U.S. Secretary of State Cordell Hull, who had been
a long-time friend and supporter of Trujillo, became
critical of the Generalissimo for the first time.
Trujillo, stung by this (and apparently realizing the
necessity of patching things up with his supporters in
the United States) decided not to run for a third term,
but instead to place the name of his Vice-President,
Jacinto Peynado, in nomination. Once again, the
Dominican Party played an important role--this time
drumming up popular enthusiasm for Peynado and turning
out the votes for Trujillo's puppet. The Party's task
was slightly more complicated this time than it had been
in 1934, as no one could show too much enthusiasm for
Peynado, as this might be interpreted as a renunciation

of Trujillo himself. The Party machinery, by now
well-established, functioned with few hitches and
Peynado was duly inaugurated as President, but not
before being publicly humiliated by Trujillo, so that
everyone would know who was still running things in the
Dominican Republic.

Through the 1940s and 1950s the Partido Dominicano
remained a faithful tool of Trujillo. Jesus de
Galindez, who paid with his life for his book critical
of the Trujillo regime, stated:

> In summary, the Dominican party has no
> doctrine, life of its own, or spontaneity, but
> it is a fundamental part of Dominican life and
> Trujillo's best instrument.[21]

Epilogue

The political history of the Dominican Republic in
the years since the assassination of Trujillo in 1961 is
well-known, but bears repeating here as a backdrop to
the fortunes of the PD in those years. The period from
1961 to 1965 was, as was inevitable, one of great disorder coupled with attempts on the part of various
groups within the nation to capture control of the
suddenly open political process. The various elements
included the civilian survivors of the Trujillo years,
headed by Joaquin Balaguer, who had been elevated to the
presidency by Trujillo in 1960 but who had, somehow,
emerged from the subsequent chaos relatively untainted
by his former associations. Another element, led by
Juan Bosch, formed a new political party--the Partido
Revolucionario Dominicano (Dominican Revolutionary Party
- PRD) in an attempt to project their own vision of the
future of the nation. The third major group was the
military, headed by a ferocious anti-communist, General
Elias Wessin y Wessin.

The extraordinary events of 1965--attempted revolution, a counter-coup by the army, and finally open
intervention by the United States--grew out of the
failure of the political process from 1961 to 1965 to
resolve the wide differences among these three groups,
plus the failure of moderate civilian elitist elements
represented by the junta which governed the country from
1963 to 1965 to come to grips with the basic political
divisions within the country.[22] Following the coup,
a provisional, non-partisan government was established
under U.S. tutelage, and began to lay the groundwork for
the election of 1966. This election was surprising in
several respects. First, almost all observers agreed
that the election was the most honest the Dominican
Republic had ever experienced. Second, Balaguer won a
surprisingly lopsided victory over Bosch and, in the

process, lay the groundwork for his domination of the Dominican political scene for the next twelve years. Although almost everyone was surprised by the Balaguer victory (less so by his subsequent victories in 1970 and 1974, as Dominican politics returned to their more familiar style of manipulation and intimidation), in retrospect and in view of what seems to be the importance of political parties in the electoral process, the victory was not surprising at all.

The post-Trujillo history of the Partido Dominicano was, in many ways, the key to understanding the political situation in the Dominican Republic. Immediately after the tyrant's assassination, the PD was excoriated by most Dominicans, along with all the other institutions associated with the hated dictatorship. The Party was officially dissolved in late 1961, never to reappear on the political scene. Balaguer had resigned as a member of the ruling civilian-military junta in January, 1961, and subsequent events sent him into exile in the United States. From there, Balaguer discerned something about the Dominican political structure that had escaped all the other participants: the political structure of the Partido Dominicano, established by Trujillo for his own selfish purposes in every small town and rural area in the Dominican Republic, was still intact![23] The PD was gone on a national scale, but at the local level the functionaries who had served the party faithfully for many years were still there, and the people were still accustomed to the Party's role of provider of both bread and circuses at the local level. Balaguer resolved to use this political machinery for his own political ends. Accordingly, in 1963, while in exile in New York, Balaguer formed the Partido Reformista (Reformist Party - PR). The party was officially recognized in Arpil, 1964, and served as Balaguer's campaign vehicle after his return to the Dominican Republic in June, 1965.

> The PR was Balaguer's personal political vehicle, organized around the president with no programs or philosophical positions beyond his individual predilections...PR members were united by loyalty to Balaguer and by mutual opportunism rather than by philosophical or policy commitments.[24]

What the author (and many others) failed to realize is that he was describing a political machine in embryo, and that political organizations based on "mutual opportunism" not only usually outlast programmatic and ideological groupings, but also produce a more fundamental political peace than do groups such as Juan Bosch's PRD. In 1966, Balaguer was described as "...the symbol of peace, tranquility, and the status quo; Bosch, the symbol of revolution."[25] Small wonder, in

retrospect, that Balaguer, with the support of the
political machinery established decades earlier by one
of the worst despots in world history, was able to
prevail in 1966 and thereafter. Trujillo had, because
of his political personality, which approximated the
bureaucratic leader ideal, established a political
structure that had outlived him. Trujillo's political
personality, like that of Plutarco Calles, approximated
Lasswell's administrators or Burns' transactional
leaders. While many of his contemporaries led through
charismatic appeals, Trujillo, through necessity and
through a life-long learning process, governed through
institutions which he could manipulate. The PD was one
of the strongest and most efficient of these institutions. In <u>Trujillismo: Genesis y Rehabilitacion,</u>
Franklin Franco suggests that the doctrine of
Trujillismo was once again being foisted on the Dominicans by Balaguer and his organization.[26] In the
sense of continuity of political organizations, he is
most assuredly correct. Balaguer, who was an extraordinary mix of scholar and politician, and who
appreciated the necessity and efficacy of political
organization, was quick to utilize the structure bequeathed him by the dead tyrant. In the 1978 presidential loss, the PR continued to show impressive
strength in other areas, barely losing control of the
Chamber of Deputies and retaining control of the Senate.
In the municipalities, the PD still retained a majority
of elected mayors, fifty-two to only thirty-two for the
PRD, now headed by the new President, Silvestre Antonio
Guzmán.[27] In the 1982 election, the PR again lost
to the PRD. With a turnout of approximately ninety percent of registered voters, Antonio Guzmán, the candidate
of the PRD, received 48.4 percent of the vote to only 37
percent for the seventy-five year old Joaquin Balaguer,
who was again the candidate of the Reformist
Party.[28] Fourteen different parties fielded eight
different candidates in the elections so, even though
the PR was now eclipsed for the second straight presidential election, it was firmly established as the
second most popular and powerful political party in the
Dominican Republic. The real test for the PR may come
in the next four years, as Balaguer's death in 1982
deprived it of its unquestioned leader. The Party must
now produce a new leader who will, as did Balaguer, take
advantage of the political machinery created in the
Dominican Republic by the tyrant, Rafael Leonidas
Trujillo.

Notes

1. Howard J. Wiarda, "The Aftermath of the Trujillo Dictatorship: The Emergence of a Pluralist Political System in the Dominican Republic," (Unpublished Ph.D. Dissertation, University of Florida, 1965, 48).
2. Dan Kurzman, "Dominican Republic," Britannica Book of the Year (Chicago: Encyclopedia Britannica, Inc., 1967), 291.
3. For a detailed analysis of the 1978 election, see G. Pope Atkins, Arms and Politics in the Dominican Republic (Boulder, Colorado: Westview Press, 1981). On the 1982 election, see various articles in the New York Times, April 2, 1982; May 17, 1982; and May 21, 1982.
4. Robert D. Crassweller, Trujillo: The Life and Times of A Caribbean Dictator (New York: The MacMillan Company, 1966), 98.
5. Selden Rodman, Quisqueya: A History of the Dominican Republic (Seattle: University of Washington Press, 1964), 113-118.
6. Ibid., p. 119.
7. The U.S. Marines evidently recognized in Trujillo someone who valued order and military discipline as much as did they. One of his former Marine commanders, Colonel Cutts, continued a friendly relation with Trujillo until 1930. See Crassweller, 68.
8. For an extensive elaboration of this thesis, see Luis F. Mejía, De Lilis a Trujillo (Caracas: Editorial Elite, 1944). In his speeches, Trujillo spoke favorably of Heureaux. His only criticism of the former caudillo was that he had not created institutions during his rule, and had therefore ultimately impoverished the political life of the nation. See Rafael L. Trujillo, Discursos, Mensajes, y Proclamas (Santiago, Dominican Republic: Editorial El Diario, 1946), Vol. I, 191.
9. Rodman, 92.
10. Ibid.
11. Pedro Andrés Pérez Cabral, La Comunidad Mulata (Caracas: Grafica Americana, 1967), 29.
12. Various biographies of Trujillo were used in the preparation of this section. The best, by far (and one of the best biographies of any Latin American leader) is Crassweller, op.cit. Others (some favorable, others unfavorable, a few more or less balanced) are: German E. Ornes, Trujillo, Little Caesar of the Caribbean (New York: Thomas Nelson and Sons, 1958); R. Emilio Jimenez, Biografia de Trujillo (Ciudad Trujillo: Editorial Caribe, 1955); Abelardo R. Nanita, Trujillo (Ciudad Trujillo: Editorial Caribe, 1954); and Jesus de Galindez, The Era of Trujillo (Tuscon, Arizona: University of Arizona Press, 1973). In addition, Trujillo's speeches and other public pronouncements are collected in an eleven-volume series, Rafael L.

Trujillo, Discursos, Mensajes, y Provlamas (Various cities in the Dominican Republic, various publishers, 1946).

13. Crassweller, 28-29.

14. Ibid.

15. Ibid., 44.

16. Trujillo, Vol. I, 10.

17. Crassweller, 99.

18. Trujillo, Vol. III, 148.

19. There are fifty-eight major references to the PD in the first seven volumes of Trujillo's collected speeches.

20. Trujillo, Vol. I, 122-123.

21. Galindez, 152.

22. The history of the immediate post-Trujillo years has been adequately chronicled by a number of authors. Among them are: Wiarda, op. cit.; Howard J. Wiarda, The Dominican Republic: Nation in Transition (New York: Frederick A. Praeger, 1969); Carlos Maria Gutierrez, El Experimento Dominicano (Mexico: Editorial Diogenes, 1974); Selden, op.cit., and Rayford Logan, Haiti and the Dominican Republic (New York: Oxford University Press, 1968).

23. Kurzman, op.cit., surprisingly, Kurzman seems to be alone in this patently obvious analysis of the 1966 election. Wiarda states, for example, "To most observers, the election results were a surprise." Wiarda, The Dominica Republic..., 197.

24. Atkins, 21.

25. Wiarda, The Dominican Republic..., 65.

26. Franklin J. Franco, Trujillismo: Genesis y Rehabilitacion (Santo Domingo: Editora Cultural Dominicana, 1971).

27. Atkins, 129.

28. New York Times, May 21, 1982, 12:5.

4
Rómulo Betancourt
and Acción Democrática

In a sense, Venezuela makes the argument for the importance of political parties in the structuring of democratic stability in Latin America. Venezuela, a country which had one of the worst political histories in Latin America from independence to the 1950s, suddenly emerged as one of the more stable democracies in the region toward the end of that decade. This democracy, replete with free elections, party competition, and a relative absence of political persecution, has continued and deepened to the present time. Party competition in presidential elections has resulted in a change of party leadership in the executive in 1963, 1968, 1973, and again in 1978; an unparalleled experience in Latin American political history. Everyone who writes about the Venezuelan democratic experience assigns a key role to the two major political parties which had their beginnings in the 1930s.[1] These two parties, Acción Democrática (Democratic Action -- AD) and the Christian Democrats (Comite de Organizacion Politica Electoral Independiente -- COPEI), have not only controlled the political process in Venezuela since 1958, but also have brought to the Venezuelan people a political democracy perhaps unequalled in Latin America. Those men responsible for the formation of Acción Democrática are called the Generation of '28, as almost all of them were students at the Central University of Venezuela in that fateful year of political awakening. COPEI was, as we shall see, founded by a later student generation -- "the Generation of '36," but the subsequent leaders of all the other major parties were of the earlier student generation. Jóvito Villalba, who participated in the founding of AD's predecessor, but who later broke with the party leadership and founded his own party, was one of the leaders of the students, as were Miguel Otero Silva, Juan Batista Fuenmajor, and Pio Tamayo, all future political leaders. Among those students who were involved in the events of the year was a second-year law student named Rómulo Betancourt, who later helped organize and bring to maturity one of the two major political parties in Venezuela - Acción Democrática.

The Environment

Venezuela in the nineteenth century knew nothing but dictatorships. First the llaneros (plainsmen) represented by Jose Antonia Paez, and later the Andinos (mountain men) represented by Cipriano Castro, ruled the nation with an iron hand. The last of the Andinos, Juan Vicente Gomez, completely dominated Venezuelan politics during his regime, 1908-1935, while at the same time certain developments were taking place that all but assured that his dictatorship would be the last of its kind in Venezuela.

Certainly, the most important development for future Venezuelan society was the beginning of the oil boom. Venezuela, which had been a backwater of Latin America for most of its national existence, was suddenly catapulted into world prominence in 1922 by the first major oil discovery in Lake Maracaibo. By the time of Gomez's death in 1935, the oil boom and the industrial expansion which followed changed fundamentally the country's society, economy, and politics. The process of social mobilization, of exposure to the modern world, began to affect people's social and political attitudes. Almost overnight, a wage-earning class was created in and around the oil fields. Further, the boom began to fuel the urbanization process, as oil began to attract hundreds of thousands of poverty-stricken farmers into the oil areas and the cities:

> Although Juan Vicente Gomez was able to prevent these social changes from having a severe impact on the country's political life so long as he was in charge, they paved the way for a substantial alteration of traditional politics in the period following his death. Then, the new classes of workers, white-collar workers, and professionals began to demand participation in public affairs.[2]

A second major change which had subsequent profound effects on Venezuelan politics was the slow but sure professionalization of the Venezuelan military under Gomez. During Gomez's rule, the Venezuelan army became a national institution, and even though it remained loyal to Gomez to the end, it would never again play the role of supporter of an individual strong man as it had in the past. After 1935, the army as an institution was a force to be reckoned with in Venezuelan politics, but Gomez had unwittingly ensured that his would-be

successors could no longer use the army as a personal
tool in their quest for power:

> At the death of Gomez in 1935, the power of the
> regional strongmen had evaporated. Castro and
> Gomez had destroyed the old system, such as it
> was, and had replaced it with autocratic cen-
> tralization. Each in his terms of office had
> reinforced central authority by the deliberate
> building of a strong national army. By the end
> of the Gomez era, the army was recognized as
> the sole road to power. Invasions on horseback
> and localized rebellions were passe.[3]

The process of institutionalization in Venezuela
did not, however, produce the same results in that
country as it did in Mexico. The Venezuelan army did
not eschew political involvement; in fact, the political
role of the army as an institution increased after
Gomez's demise. The difference between the two
countries appears to stem from the lack of an expanding
civilian (or at least ex-military) elite who held
political power and were capable of co-opting the military, as Obregón, Calles, and Cárdenas did in Mexico.
In Venezuela, on the contrary, once the age of the
caudillos had ended, the nation was immediately ushered
into a new age of army dominance of the political
process -- a dominance that lasted until the decisive
civilian triumph of 1957. Even so, the Venezuelan military still plays an important role in the nation's
political process.[4]

By the 1930s, however, the role of the military had
undergone a definitive change, and after 1935, civilian
political leaders had much more room to maneuver than
they had before that year. New civilian elites,
especially the university-educated professional class
located predominantly in Caracas, now had a chance to
participate at the edges of the political process.

The change in the political atmosphere in Venezuela
was due as much to changed personalities among the new
military leaders of the nation as it was to the changing
economic and social environment of the nation. The two
army generals who ruled Venezuela from 1936 to 1945 were
a far cry from the caudillos who had preceded them. The
first, Brigadier General Eleazar Lopez Contreras, had
been Minister of War under Gomez at the time of his
death, and was the unanimous choice of the cabinet to
finish the presidential term, which expired in 1936.
Lopez was then duly elected for a new seven-year term
(shortened to five by a constitutional change insisted
upon by Lopez), and then in 1941, turned over the reigns
of government to yet another army general, Isaias Medina
Angarita, elected in a peaceful if somewhat fraudulent
election. Both these men were Andinos, from the State

of Tachira, which had provided the two great caudillos
of the twentieth century. Yet both were quite different
in temperament and political orientation from Castro and
Gomez. Lopez had been the person within the Gomez
regime most responsible for the professionalization of
the armed forces, and was extremely popular within the
army, as well as among key civilian elements. Lopez,
then, provided a transition between "the stultifying
dictatorship of Juan Vicente Gomez and the liberal
regime of Isaias Medina Angarita, his immediate
successor."[5] The reflexive actions of the old dictatorship were gone, and in their stead was a new type of
military regime which tolerated some dissent, but which
still drew the line at actions it believed would under-
mine continued military rule:

> At times, President Lopez Contreras was tough
> and implacable; at others, he was tolerant and
> permissive. He committed himself to disman-
> tling the machinery of the Gomez tyranny, but
> as a realist, he was aware of the risks
> inherent in trying to establish a wide-open
> democratic regime immediately on the heels of
> the longest and most oppressive dictatorship in
> Venezuelan history. He succeeded, with his
> gradualism, in rationalizing and humanizing
> Venezuelan government and, to a degree, in
> separating the military from the civilian
> government.[6]

The period from 1936 to 1941, then, was a period of
profound political and social change in Venezuela. Deep
forces, such as the changes wrought by the oil boom,
concatenated with the personalities of the time. As the
military changed, so did the civilian sector. The
"Generation of '28", referred to earlier, had been so
named because they, as university students, had
presented perhaps the most serious opposition to the
Gomez regime in 1928. The so-called student week of
February of that year had escalated into a major
manifestation of anti-Gomez feeling, and had been met
with force by the regime of the old tyrant. Nevertheless, the student leaders at the time had survived, even
if from exile, and had returned to Venezuela immediately
after Gomez's death. They now turned to the task of
organizing civilian political groups, and the late
1930s in Venezuela were characterized by a plethora of
nascent political associations. The old student
organization, the Federacion de Estudiantes Venezolanos
(Venezuelan Student Federation -- FEV) was reorganized,
and immediately began championing the cause of democracy
in Venezuela. The list of political organizations
included the moderate Union Nacional Republicana
(National Republican Union -- UNR), which had several of

its members elected to the new Congress. The Partido
Republicano Progresista (Progressive Republican Party --
PRP) soon fell under communist influence and was subsequently outlawed by the Lopez administration. Other
minor political groupings, some based on class lines and
some on regional identity, were also organized during
the period. The major national, multi-class group to
emerge from the relative freedom of the late 1930s was
Organizacion Venezolana (Venezuelan Organization --
ORVE). Its founders were almost all members of the
"Generation of '28" and included such former student
leaders as Raul Leoní, Luis Beltrán Figueroa, Gonzalo
Barrios, and Romulo Betancourt. ORVE was in reality a
popular front which sought to bring together diverse
elements into one political organizaton. The organizers of ORVE, especially Betancourt, made the immediate
decision to, in the words of the intellectual Mariano
Picon-Salas, "look for what unites us and to avoid what
divides us."[7] The subsequent history of ORVE during
the late years of the 1930s is largely one of repeated
attempts to gain legal status, and to combine with other
groups on the non-communist left to form a united
political party, known as the Partido Democratico
Nacional (National Democratic Party -- PDN). Finally,
on March 13, 1937, after a period in which the new
political groupings on the left had made substantial
gains during the congressional elections in February of
that year, President Lopez Contreras ordered the
expulsion of forty-seven of the new opposition leaders.
Thus ended the first attempt at legality for the
"Generation of '28."
    For the next four years, the civilian opponents of
continued military rule were forced to work clandestine-
ly. At the same time, Lopez Contreras was proving to be
a consummate politician. Utilizing a deft combination
of harassment of and accommodation with his opponents,
Lopez Contreras managed to maintain control of
Venezuelan politics. As the years wore on, however,
Lopez became more lenient, and efforts to organize the
PDN increased. Finally, Lopez decided to hold elections
in 1941, and to use the indirect elections as a means of
passing power to a new president, Minister of War,
Isaias Medina Angarita. In spite of the rigged nature
of the elections, the PDN decided to field a candidate
for president, none other than the famed Venezuelan
novelist, Rómulo Gallegos. Gallegos immediately
embarked on a nationwide speaking tour, and proved
himself to be an excellent campaigner in a losing cause,
thereby setting the stage for his subsequent accession
to the presidency. Further, the campaign set in motion
events which led to the founding, only three months
later, of Acción Democrática (Democratic Action -- AD)
as the first mass-based, civilian-led party in
Venezuela. The initial policy statements of AD, and its

application for legal recognition from the government, were kept deliberately vague so as to forestall any governmental pretext for non-recognition. This time, changed circumstances and changed personalities led to recognition of the new party, and on Saturday, September 13, 1941, Acción Democrática was officially constituted in a public meeting in Caracas. Prominent among those who spoke at the initial meeting was Romulo Betancourt, who had recently returned from a two-year exile in Chile, after having eluded the Lopez Contreras police for the preceding two years while serving as Organizational Secretary for the PDN.

The first task facing the leaders of the new party was organization, and they leapt to the task. Betancourt, especially, because of his prior two years' experience during the clandestine period, was well-suited for the task, and immediately assumed a position of leadership within the party. First, the party's national organization was strengthened and deepened, to reflect the new legal status of the party. New offices, including feminine and youth secretariats, were created so that the party might carry its appeal to these groups. A new Comite Directivo Nacional (National Directive Committee -- CDN) was also established, in order to give the regional leaders, who were to play a major role in the party's future successes, a major voice in party councils. New organizations were also created at the regional and local levels in order to increase the party's appeal.

All of thse efforts at organization paid off sooner than expected. As the elections of 1945 approached, a great deal of maneuvering over presidential succession began, still within the context of an indirect vote for the new president. Medina was loath to choose Lopez Contreras as his successor, even though the former president wanted very much to return to the office he had vacated four years earlier for his fellow army officer and Andino. After a series of pre-electoral maneuvers, in which Medina tried to tread a path between the Lopecistas on the one hand and the civilians on the other, the President announced that the official government candidate for president would be Angel Biaggini, the Minister of Agriculture. It was apparent that Medina had chosen a colorless, powerless government official in an attempt to rule through his chosen puppet. It was at this point that AD became involved with a group of junior military officers in plotting the coup that, in October, 1945, overthrew the Medina government and ushered in a brief but open period of democracy for Venezuela.

The new junta which now governed the country was composed of two of the military officers who had plotted the coup, an independent civilian, and four members of Acción Democrática -- provisional president Rómulo

Betancourt, Raul Leoni, Luis B. Prieto, and Gonzalo Barrios. As the provisional government, dominated by AD, began to prepare the country for the first direct elections it had ever experienced, AD began to enter a new phase. For the first time, the major opposition was not the military, but several other new political parties which had also organized during the 1930s. Foremost among these was the aforementioned COPEI, but also in the field were the Venezuelan Communist Party (PCV) and Union Republicana Democratica (Democratic Republican Union -- URD) under the leadership of Jóvito Villalba.

One of Betancourt's first political acts after the coup was to declare that no member of the junta could or would become a candidate for the presidency. This was a master stroke, as it deprived the opposition of a major campaign issue -- that of continuismo -- but left in the field perhaps the strongest AD candidate -- Rómulo Gallegos.

The first elections held after the coup were for a constituent assembly to create a new constitution. They were widely regarded as a test of AD's popularity and AD emerged as the triumphant winner, with almost 80 percent of the vote. COPEI was a distant second, and the PCV and URD trailed badly. Under the new (1947) constitution, duly written by the constituent assembly, AD swept the congressional elections in December, 1947, with over 70 percent of the vote. Gallegos and AD scored a triumphant victory in the presidential race on the same day, with Gallegos receiving almost 75 percent of the vote. Once again, COPEI and its candidate, Rafael Caldera, were a distant second.

In spite of its shining electoral successes, AD was faced with severe problems which taxed the leadership capabilities of what was a thin group of experienced politicians at the national level. A major problem, as it turned out, was simply numbers. AD membership had swelled from about 75,000 in 1941 to almost half a million by 1948. The leadership was, in many instances, inundated by sheer numbers. In some instances, also, new recruits came more for the money and prestige that they assumed would be theirs, than for the opportunity to work for the party. Further, after 1945, the party leadership had had to govern as well as run the party, and this double task inevitably took away from their party efforts:

> The party was still a young and sprawling organization by no means sufficiently equipped or experienced to operate and institute the far-reaching national revolution envisioned by its leadership. In many ways it was clearly in a state of adolescence, with maturity well into the future. Given a different set of circum-

stances, the AD might have weathered the years
ahead, as did Mexico's PRI after years of turmoil and bloodshed. However, the Venezuelan
political environment proved too much for the
ardent young revolutionaries. The result was
the November 1948 counter-revolution which
swept Acción Democrática from power, relegat-
ing it to a decade of exile while bringing to
the Venezuelan people a superficial prosperity
which failed to hide a politically corrupt,
socially unenlightened despotism under military
direction.[8]

The new military dictatorship that took over in
late 1948 was implacably opposed to the AD, regarding it
as its major enemy in the country. Accordingly, the
period from 1948 to 1958 when at last the dictatorship
of Marcos Perez Jimenez was overthrown by yet another
coup designed to bring about civilian government, was
one of enforced exile for many Adecos and underground
activity for those who remained in Venezuela.[9] Given
the circumstances, AD's goals during the period were
minimal: maintain a skeletal national and local
organization, while at the same time engaging in
political introspection and planning for the future.
That the party succeeded in its goals is clear from the
post-1958 history of Venezuelan politics. However, what
also became clear after the first euphoric years of
civilian (and AD) rule had passed was that new problems
had been created within the party as a result of this
second period of enforced clandestine status. Foremost
among the new problems was factionalism, based primarily
on an ideological and political distance between the
Guardia Vieja (Old Guard) and a younger group of Adecos
known as the arsistas. Eventually, this factionalism
was to produce openings for COPEI, and to produce the
two-party system which today characterizes Venezuelan
politics. However, AD did successfully weather the
storm of the ten-year dictatorship, although this time
almost all the party leaders, including Betancourt, were
forced into exile.

Party activities during the first months after the
1958 coup were frantic. The governing junta, headed by
former Rear Admiral Wolfgang Larrazabal, had promised
free elections later in the year, and these were held in
December. In the meantime, the party returned to the
activity it knew best: organization. The National
Executive Committee met in early January, and immediately set about reconstituting the party's command structure down to the local level. There was a realization
at the time that the upcoming election would depend as
much or more on party organization as on ideological
positions, so that was, as always, where the energies
were directed. The party's first national convention

after the dictatorship was finally held in August, and Betancourt was named President of the National Executive Committee, with Gallegos as Honorary President. The Party's position on the upcoming elections was somewhat equivocal: they were willing to consider the possibility of either a unity candidate with all the non-communist parties, or possibly a collegiate executive, but failing agreement on these two possibilities, the AD would field its own candidate, Romulo Betancourt.

Events during the next few months made the first two courses impossible, so on October 11, Betancourt's candidacy was announced by the AD National Directive Committee. The subsequent campaign was hectic, but devoid of extremism. The AD campaign was the best organized, but Larrazabal, who had consented to run as the candidate for the URD, exhibited a surprisingly magnetic appeal, especially in and around Caracas, where he had become something of a folk-hero. When the votes were finally counted several days after the election, Betancourt and AD had gained almost fifty percent of the votes, with Larrazabal a strong second. Larrazabal actually swept Caracas by a large margin, and it was only AD's organizational strength in the interior that gave it the victory. After a few days of uncertainty, with some violence in Caracas, Larrazabal took to tele- vision and radio in an appeal for public order and respect for the electoral results. Rómulo Betancourt and Acción Democrática, the party he helped found, became the new popularly elected leaders of a Venezuela entering what now appears to be a period of unprece- dented and (at the time) unexpected democratic stabi- lity. Since 1958, as AD and other parties, especially COPEI have matured, and as successive schisms within AD have reduced its initial majority status in the country, Venezuela has been treated to a twenty-five year period of intense party competition that has resulted in regular five-year changes in party dominance. Although Betancourt was followed in the presidency in 1963 by another Adeco, Raul Leoní; in 1968 Rafael Caldera, the founder of COPEI, was elected president. In 1973, Carlos Andres Peréz, the candidate of AD, swept into office, with nearly fifty percent of the vote. Pérez' victory signaled something else for AD: a generational change in party leadership. Pérez was not a member of the Guardia Vieja faction of the Party, and his election signaled that AD was revitalizing its leadership with younger people, a certain sign of increasing institu- tionalization within the Party.

The elections of 1978 again brought a political turnabout, as COPEI candidate Luis Herrera Campins won the presidency and COPEI gained control of the Congress. An internal debate within the AD as a result of this electoral loss, plus an even more embarrassing loss in subsequent municipal elections, brought yet another

generation of positions of power within the Party, as
Andres Perez lost ground within party councils. As this
is being written, Venezuelans are once again getting
ready to participate in what has now become for them
routine: a free election for both President and Congress, to be held as scheduled in December, 1983. At
the moment it appears likely that the AD candidate,
James Lusinchi, will win, even though COPEI's nominee is
former president Rafael Caldera, who wants to be the
only man twice elected to the presidency. From the
overall perspective of Latin American politics, however,
the important point is not who will win in December, but
that free elections have now become almost routine in
Venezuela, and that the key element in this process has
been the emergence of an institutionalized political
party known as Acción Democrática. The political
leadership role played by Rómulo Betancourt in the
founding and development of that Party was a crucial
part of this process.

The Leader

For a number of reasons, more has been written on
the life and political thought of Rómulo Betancourt than
almost any other Latin American political leader. He
became, in the early 1960s, the symbol of President John
F. Kennedy's Alliance for Progress, and its announced
goal of restoring democratic government in Latin
America. Because AD has been so successful within the
context of Venezuelan politics, several excellent books
chronicling the rise of the Party have been written, and
Betancourt's role in the process has been duly
recounted. Further, Betancourt and Acción Democrática
have, down through the years, exerted a profound
influence on North American social scientists, as sort
of a rare flower in the otherwise arid soil of Latin
American militarism and personalism. As John D. Martz
stated in his masterful work on Acción Democrática, "The
successful survival of the AD in the face of recent
factionalsim and inner disunity suggests a lengthy
future for a party that has established itself as one of
the most prominent in the hemisphere."[10] Finally,
Betancourt himself has been an apt subject for political
biography. Unlike many Latin American political
leaders, his life is relatively easy to chronicle,
possibly because of the open nature of the man himself.
Betancourt lived in the United States during his 1948-
1958 exile, and this stay produced friendships with
several academics here, most notably Robert J. Alexander
of Rutgers University. Alexander's book Romulo Betancourt and the Transformation of Venezuela is an
outstanding political biography. Finally, there does
not appear, as was the case with both Calles in Mexico

and Trujillo in the Dominican Republic, any attempt to
obscure facts and events, especially of family background, that might detract from the Great Man in
politics.

Although Rómulo Betancourt's life from 1928 on was
that of a man caught up in the political toils of the
time, his early childhood gave little or no indication
of this penchant for politics. Betancourt was born in
1908 in the little town of Guatire, in the State of
Miranda, to the east of Caracas. His father, Luis
Betancourt, was an immigrant from the Canary Islands,
who had arrived in Venezuela during the last years of
the nineteenth century. He was self-educated, and at
the time of Rómulo's birth was manager of a small town
enterprise, that offered various services, including a
restaurant, store, drugstore, and banking services to
the local gentry. Rómulo's mother had been born in the
Guatire region, but part of her family had also come
from the Canary Islands. Rómulo's childhood was not
extraordinary, except that his father possessed several
characteristics which were not all that common in
Guatire. One was a penchant for hard work and long
hours, while another was an insistence on punctuality.
Although Luis died when Rómulo was not yet in his teens,
this fatherly influence carried over into later life,
when hard work, organization, and punctuality became
hallmarks of the political leader.

A major influence on young Rómulo Betancourt was
his teacher in the Guatire primary school, a young man
named Juan Jose Fermin. Fermin was an unconventional
teacher for the times, rejecting the rote approach to
learning which was then in vogue. Instead, Fermin
utilized innovative approaches to education, which
included what today we would label experiential learning. Rómulo, among others, was induced to get out of
the classroom to find out what was going on around him,
and this too left his mark in later years.

Perhaps more important than what actually occurred
in Guatire is what Betancourt remembered about his
childhood. Guatire evidently appeared to be idyllic to
him in later years. The order and the organization,
coupled with the fun of his early childhood seem to have
left stong impressions on the man.

When Betancourt had finished grammar school, his
parents moved to Caracas, where he entered the Liceo
Caracas, preparatory to enrolling at the Central
University of Venezuela (Universidad Central de
Venezuela -- UCV). Here he came under the influence of
Rómulo Gallegos, who later was to become Venezuela's
most famous man of letters and also the first president
of the AD. Undoubtedly, much of Betancourt's interest
in politics came from the Venezuelan intellectual who,
in the best Latin American tradition, was also deeply
interested in politics. During the time in the Liceo,

Betancourt worked at two part-time jobs to help pay his tuition at the school. Upon receiving his <u>bachillerato,</u> the young student enrolled at the UCV in the latter part of 1926, and it was here that he encountered the other members of what became known as the "Generation of '28."

The events of February, 1928, which ultimately led to a total re-structuring of Venezuelan politics, began innocently enough with the Venezuelan Student Federation declaring a student week which was to be a literary and social event. During the week, several speeches critical of the Gomez dictatorship were given, and several marches in open defiance of the regime occurred. Gomez reacted by arresting most of the student leaders of the FEV, including Rómulo Betancourt. Public re-action, however, was intense and the students were soon released, but then began plotting a coup. The coup, which was to prove abortive, took place in April. It was poorly planned from the beginning, and was a dismal failure. Many of the participants were shot, others were jailed, and Betancourt was forced into the first of several exiles, this one to last for eight years until the death of Gomez in 1935. According to Alexander:

> The April 1928 plot was a failure. However, it contributed to the political education of the students who participated in it. It helped convince them that the overthrow of Gomez' and the caudillo system would be the result of a long and patient effort, rather of a one-night adventure.[11]

Betancourt's subsequent political life was from then on inextricably entwined with his personal life. It becomes almost impossible to divide the two after 1928. The years in exile -- 1928-1935, 1939-1941, and 1948-1958 -- were all spent in promoting or assuring the continuance of the various political organizations back in Venezuela. First ORVE, then the PDN, and finally AD became the consuming passions of his life. The years in Venezuela were spent in even more feverish organization-al activity. Betancourt became, successively, a member of the top leadership of ORVE, Organization Secretary of the PDN, Organization Secretary of the AD, and finally the Party's president. He was, whatever his post, always recognized as the organizer, even though his speaking ability was far superior to that of either Calles or Trujillo. Betancourt exuded a charisma that would have taken him far in politics in any event, but he was convinced that only organization would produce the kinds of permanent changes in Venezuelan politics he hoped for.

Perhaps the most fecund organizational period for the AD, and one which stood it in good stead during its subsequent ten years of persecution, was the period of legality from 1941 to 1948. This was the period in which AD attempted to take its central organization to the countryside, in a massive campaign aimed at creating a Party organization in every municipality in Venezuela. Betancourt, who participated enthusastically in this process, has written almost lyrically of the times:

> 1941-1945 was a four-year period that left an indelible impression. In my youthful exile I had always wanted to know the immensity of Venezuela, town by town, hamlet by hamlet; to look within and to live with its problems; to discuss its destiny with men and women of the plains and of the mountains; of the Oriente and of Guayana. I achieved that secret desire in years that taught me much more of my country than I would have learned through book study.[12]

During the period of 1948 to 1958, Betancourt again was the organizer, maintaining the Party's underground organization for the day when the new dictatorship would come to an end. He remained President of AD during the decenio of the dictatorship and was the major figure in AD's Coordinating Committee in Exile.

After the fall of Pérez Jimenez, Betancourt once again was able to practice his organizational abilities in Venezuela, and largely as a result of his efforts, AD has survived several internal schisms, a generational change in leadership, the loss of two elections to its arch-rival, COPEI, and remains today one of the best-institutionalized political parties in Latin America. John Martz has referred to Betancourt as "the organizational genius of Acción Democrática." In Martz's words:

> ...the importance of AD among the parties of Latin America is its reliance upon organization. Furthermore, it has been this, the machinery of the AD, that more than any other single factor has been responsible for the succession of electoral victories throughout the years.... The original leaders of the movement that became AD recognized the need for a truly national party, with organs and representatives extending to the most remote parts of the Republic.... Leaders of the party are especially proud of the fact that the party rather than the person is placed first.[13]

If, as the Venezuelan writer Manuel Vicente Magallanes states, "In the modern state, political parties have attained the category of necessary institutions,"[14] then the activities of the "Generation of '28" led by Rómulo Betancourt, have been indispensable

in ending military rule and bringing democratic government to the people of Venezuela. Venezuelan politics
are, by concensus, the politics of a two-party dominant
system, with Acción Democrática and COPEI vying openly
for power in freely contested, regular elections.
Perhaps the greatest political success story in Latin
America is Romulo Betancourt and Acción Democrática in
Venezuela.

Notes

1. See, for example, Robert J. Alexander, Rómulo Betancourt and the Transformation of Venezuela (New Brunswick, NJ: Transaction Books, 1982); John D. Martz, Acción Democrática: Evolution of a Modern Political Party (Princeton, NJ: Princeton University Press, 1966); and Manuel Vicente Magallanes, Partidos Politicos Venezolanos (Caracas: Tipografia Vargas, 1959).

2. Alexander, 14-15.

3. Winfield J. Burrggraaff, The Venezuelan Armed Forces in Politics (Columbia, MO: University of Missouri Press, 1972).

4. Frank Bonilla, A Strategy for Research On Social Policy (Cambridge, MA: MIT Press, 1967), 286ff.

5. Burrggraaff, 33.

6. Ibid.

7. Martz, 29.

8. Martz, 80.

9. Alexander, 145.

10. Major sources used in relating the life of Betancourt include: Alexander; Martz; Robert J. Alexander, The Venezuelan Democratic Revolution: A Profile of the Regime of Romulo Betancourt (New Brunswick, Rutgers University Press, 1964); Luis Cordero Vasquez, Betancourt y la Conjura Militar del 45 (Caracas: n.p., 1978); Luis Gonzalez Herrera, Romulo en Berna: Un Documento Para la Historia de Accion Democratica (Caracas: Editorial Centauro, 1978); Juan Liscano, Multimagen de Romulo: Vida y Accion de Romulo Betancourt en Graficas (Caracas: Orbeca, 1978); Jose Luis Rangel (ed.), Romulo, el General Betancourt y Otros Escritos (Caracas: Editorial Centauro, 1971); Arturo Sosa Abascal, Del Garibaldismo Estudiantil a la Izquierda Criolla (Caracas, Editorial Centauro, 1981); Ramon J. Velasquez, Betancourt en la Historia de Venezuela del Siglo XX (Caracas: Editorial Centauro, 1980); Vigencia y Proyeccion de Romulo: 50 Años de Liderazgo Politico (Caracas: Partido Accion Democratica, 1978).

11. Alexander, The Transformation of Venezuela, 42-43.

12. Romulo Betancourt, Venezuela: Politica y Petroleo (Caracas, n.p., 1967), 135-136.

13. Martz, 147.

14. Magallanes, 11.

Part 3
The Failures

Unfortunately for the current political peace of Latin America a number of countries have failed to produce political parties that have, for a long period of time, dominated or controlled the electoral process. In each of the countries we will examine (Argentina, Chile, Cuba, and Peru) a mass-based political party was founded, enjoyed initial success in attracting adherents (and in two of the four cases actually gained power via the ballot box), but eventually failed to consolidate their early successes. In each case, but for different reasons as we shall see, the ultimate failure must be linked overwhelmingly to the persona of the party leader, even though he also played an important role. Anyone reading these pages must at times want to stop and say, "How could you do it?" How could Yrigoyen, Alessandri, Grau San Martin, and Haya de la Torre let the opportunity to build leading political institutions slip through their grasp? How could they fritter away the tremendous popularity which they and their party enjoyed? How could they, all intelligent men, fail to perceive what lay within their grasp if only they would act wisely? Some will say that the opportunities appear only in hindsight, but the opportunities were so clear, so compelling at the time that even men of lesser vision than these saw the chance to build. Yet these men, with their political acumen, their political success, their control over millions of adherents, let it all slip through their grasp, and in the end the political process in their nations came to be dominated by varying combinations of chaos, terrorism and military rule.

5
Hipólito Yrigoyen and the Unión Cívica Radical

Argentina is the most perplexing and frustrating country in Latin America. Located in the south tempe- rate zone, Argentina is one of the wealthier countries in Latin America. Moreover, it has been a rich country for some time. Walt W. Rostow estimates that Argentina was the one Latin American country to pass his mythical "take-off" into self-sustained economic growth in the 1920s. Moreover, Argentina is blessed with bountiful natural resources, a literate and well trained popu- lation, racial homogeneity, and a good transportation system, in short, all of the factors necessary to create a modern nation. In many ways, in fact, Argentina is a modern nation, when compared to many other Latin American nations. Yet, in spite of all its material abundance, Argentina remains one of the most violent and repressive nations in all of Latin America. Since 1930, the army has ruled the country for more than 75 percent of the time. From 1943 to 1955, Argentina experienced what was perhaps the first fascist dictatorship in Latin American history--that of Juan and Evita Peron. Until 1983, the army continued its rule, having killed or abducted uncounted thousands of its own citizens, some of whom dared to challenge its continued domination of the country. Reportage on Argentina continually empahsizes the disillusionment and pervading cynicism of the Argentines toward politics. It was as if the social contract did not exist in Argentina. There was no sense of belonging to a nation, only an all pervading sense of a war of all against all. Argentina probably came as close as we can come in the real world to the state of man in nature envisioned by Thomas Hobbes.
Argentina is especially frustrating for the politi- cal scientist interested in the process of national development. He knows that, according to Lipset, economic development and legitimacy are the two pre- requisites for stable democracy. He knows, further, that Argentina possesses all of the demographic material and attributes to qualify as a "developed" nation, and

that democracy is an almost exclusive preserve of the
economically developed nations of the world. What,
then, has gone wrong? Here is where an interesting
dichotomy appears. For most non-Argentine writers,
Argentina's problems began with the dictatorship of Juan
and Evita Peron. They were the people who irrevocably
split the nation between the old guard and the army on
the one hand, and organized labor and the descamisados
on the other. Argentina's political problems since 1955
are traced, then, to the continuing struggle between the
conservative old guard and the Peronistas for the
political soul of the nation. The army has the guns and
the Peronistas have the masses: Thus the continuing
bloody confrontation. On the other hand, when Argentines write their own political history a different
story emerges. It is no accident that there are more
books published in the Argentine on Hipolito Yrigoyen
than on Juan Peron. The Argentines perceive a truth
about their own political failures that non-Argentines
often miss: the seeds for the current and continuing
political and social malaise in Argentina were sown, not
in the 1950s, but in the 1920s; and not by the Perons
but by Hipólito Yrigoyen. Argentina's problems have
more to do with Yrigoyen's decimation of the Unión
Cívica Radical in the 1920s than they do with the creation of the Peronista party in the 1950s. As we shall
see, the UCR had become by the 1920s the balance wheel
of Argentine politics. It had its roots in the nineteenth century, came to power in the elections of 1916
under the leadership of its charismatic leader,
Yrigoyen, and by the early 1920s had taken on the attributes of a modern, mass-based political party, with wide
appeal among the emerging Argentine middle class. It
looked as if the UCR would continue to dominate the
Argentine political process for years to come. The
party had organization, leadership, program, and an
appealing ideology. It had come to power at just the
time that the Argentine middle class had begun to assert
itself politically. The concatenation of party and
changing social environment was "right" for the future
development of a modern party and party system in
Argentina. If ever the sociological conditions for
party development were fulfilled in Latin America,
Argentina was the place and the 1920s were the time. In
spite of all this promise, however, by 1930 the whole
political edifice had collapsed and the army, which had
assumed a relatively apolitical role in recent years,
was in control of the government. In reality, Argentina
has had no political democracy and little political
peace since that time. What went wrong? The
environment was propitious, but the crucial element of
political leadership was missing. Instead of a Calles,
a Betancourt, or even a Trujillo, Argentina and the UCR
were cursed with a charismatic destroyer of institutions

and of political peace--Hipólito Yrigoyen.

The Environment

By the 1920s, Argentina had almost completed the process of national development, begun in the late nineteenth century, that made it the most modern and economically advanced nation in Latin America. The Argentine economy was tied to a mammoth export sector, centered on beef and wool. By the 1920s, Argentina was one of the ten greatest trading nations in the world, exporting the agricultural products of its incredibly rich pampas to the industrialized European nations, primarily Great Britain. At the same time, a slow increase in manufacturing, much of it tied to the agricultural sector, decreased the nation's dependence on imported manufactured goods; although approximately forty percent of all such goods were still being imported. Income distribution, although improving slightly as some of the wealth generated by exports trickled down to the lower sectors of society, remained skewed toward the rich. One reason for the continued imbalance was the failure of labor to organize, so that workers had little political influence with succeeding governments. Even so, Argentine workers in the 1920s were better off than their colleagues in any other Latin American country, in terms of their living standards.

A concomitant of economic development seems to be increased urbanization. In the case of Argentina, urbanization began early. By 1914, over fifty percent of Argentina's population lived in urban areas. Argentina was the first Latin American nation to have over half its population living in urban areas. Buenos Aires was, of course, the major city, with a population of over 2 million, about 25 percent of the total population. Other interior cities, such as Tucuman and Cordoba, grew at a rapid rate during the period. Along with increased urbanization came increased literacy. National literacy was more than 60 percent in 1914, even though it was concentrated in urban areas. Education had become secular in Argentina in 1884, when the decision was made to provide free public primary education.

During the period 1890-1914, the middle class, especially the urban middle class, increased rapidly. Estimates are that by 1914 the middle class constituted over 30 percent of the population of Buenos Aires, enormous by Latin American standards of the day. At the same time, Argentina was experiencing a demographic phenomenon almost unknown in the rest of Latin America: large numbers of immigrants were finding their way to its shores. By 1930, 31 percent of Argentina's population was foreign-born, more than twice the percentage ever reached in the United States. Mainly as a result of this immigration, the population of Argentina expanded rapidly from 1890 to 1930. Total population went from 3.9 million in 1895 to 11.2 million in 1930, giving Argentina one of the fastest rates of population growth in Latin America. In short, the period from 1890 to 1930 was a golden age for Argentina. Economically and socially, the nation was surging toward modernity, and the vision of the limitless pampa, with all its riches, and of the cosmopolitan Buenos Aires, with its striking similarity to the great cities of Europe, seemed to presage a glorious future for this first "modern" Latin American nation.

All of the social and economic changes during the period seemed to favor political change as well. Argentina was, at least on the surface, a textbook case of a society ready for the emergence of modern political parties. Literacy and urbanization brought with them increased social mobilization and increased demands for participation in the political process by the middle class. Economic development, even though uneven, led to an ever-expanding middle class, plus an ever-larger urban proletariat that also began to make some political demands on the system. Argentina was facing, during the period, a crisis of participation in the political system, and it appeared that the system was responding in a positive way to this crisis, through the development of not one but two broad-based political parties with mass appeal. Organized in the late nineteenth century, both the Argentine Socialist Party and the Unión Cívica Radical increasingly challenged continued rule by the old conservative oligarchy. After the electoral reforms of 1912, electoral participation by the masses increased, and the victory of the UCR in the 1916 presidential elections seemed to portend a new era in Argentine politics. Much of the credit for the changed political circumstances was due to the statesmanship of the last conservative President, Roque Saenz Peña, who both imposed the electoral reform law in 1912, and made it stick until he fell ill in 1913. Fortunately, the Vice President, Victorino de la Plaza, who took over for the unexpired portion of Saenz Peña's term, also believed in the electoral reform, and efforts by the conservatives to subvert the new law were thwarted. The reform, known to this day by the name of the former president who proposed it, provided for males over eighteen an obligatory, free, and secret vote. It also provided for a division of the seats in the Chamber of Deputies between the two political parties with the largest vote totals, thereby ensuring a type of minority representation in the Congress, even though the Senate was still chosen by the Provincial governments.

The Saenz Peña electoral reform provided the conditions necessary for a Radical breakthrough in the elections of 1916. In that election Yrigoyen was the

overwhelming choice as candidate of the UCR, and won the
presidency with a comfortable majority of the popular
vote, and a slim majority of the electoral vote. His
inauguration was the scene of one of the most joyous
celebrations in the history of Buenos Aires:

> As Yrigoyen came from the inauguration cere-
> mony, the crowd took the horses from his
> carriage and pulled it themselves through the
> rejoicing city. There was a sense that the
> milennium had been reached. Women threw
> flowers from balconies on the hope of a new and
> better if not too well-defined Argentina. Sad
> to say, only fourteen years later, ladies would
> be throwing flowers from balconies to soldiers
> marching through the streets to remove Yrigoyen
> from office.[1]

The political party which Yrigoyen represented and
which he had helped nurture to its present position of
power had been organized officially in 1891, and had
grown out of several currents in Argentine life. The
most immediate cause for the creation of the new
political party was the financial crisis of the late
1880s, which cast doubts upon the continuing ability of
the conservative leadership to manage the economy
successfully. The growing number of middle class
reformers in and around Buenos Aires had found much to
their dismay that appeals for changes in the political
system, which they regarded as an anachronism when
compared with Argentina's economic and social modernization, had fallen largely upon deaf ears so long as
the economy continued to boom. The financial disaster
of 1887-1889, however, made the appeals of these would-
be reformers more palatable to many, combined as they
were with anger at economic losses and obvious mis-
management of the economy by the oligarchy. Foremost
among these reformers, who wanted a free and honest
political system, was Leandro Alem. Aided by his
nephew, Hipólito Yrigoyen, Alem had attempted to work
against the regime of Juarez Celman, a relative of
former president, Julio Roca, within the apparatus of
the Partido Autonoma Nacional (National Autonomous
Party--PAN). The PAN was a loose coalition of
establishment figures, including Roca himself, who were
interested in reforming the establishment so that it
could continue to rule. Only Alem and a few other
younger members saw the overthrow of the conservative
elite as both a necessity and a possibility.
Consequently, they had little influence within the party
itself, and founded a series of evanescent political
clubs, which were really debating societies for the new
ideas emanating from this group, As always, the young
were also in the forefront of those opposing continued

oligarchic rule; in part because ex-president Bartolome
Mitre, a hero of the anticonservative elements, kept
emphasizing the leading role the youth must play in any
political regeneration of the Argentine nation.

In addition to the middle-aged politicians and the
largely university-educated youth, a small group of
junior army officers was also willing to act against the
regime. Communication was established between the army
group and the civilians, who were now organized into the
Unión Cívica de Juventud (Civic Union of Youth--UCJ)
with Alem at its head. After several meetings, the UCJ
became simply the Unión Cívica (Civic Union--UC) with
Alem as its leader. The immediate result of all this
political organizing and meetings with the junior army
officers was minimal: an abortive coup attempt in July,
1890, eventually led to the resignation of Juarez, but
that was probably just as fervently desired by his
conservative allies as by the new groups. By Juarez's
resignation, the oligarchy actually consolidated its
position by removing the incompetent President.
Further, divisions within the Unión Cívica began to
appear, as the followers of ex-president Mitre split
with Alem and his group, with the former labeling Alem
as a radical. The result was that Alem and his
colleagues, including Yrigoyen formed the Unión Cívica
Radical, soon to be known simply as the Radical Party,
in 1892. From that time on the UCR was the major institution representing the growing Argentine middle class
in the political process of the nation.

Still, the UCR was to undergo a long period of
political failure before its eventual electoral success
in 1916. For twenty-six years, from 1890 to 1916, the
conservative elite maintained political control of the
nation. During this period the UCR, which came increasingly under the control of Yrigoyen, adopted several
tactics in its attempts to gain power. Yrigoyen himself
was involved in coup attempts, not only in 1890 but
again in 1893 and in 1905. Each time the attempt
failed, both because the Radicals did not have the
necessary support among the junior officers of the army
and because the growing middle class had not yet
sufficiently identified with the Radical cause to give
them broad popular support. A second tactic adopted by
Yrigoyen was abstention from elections. The UCR leadership hoped that, by refusing to participate in what were
viewed as rigged elections, they would both call
attention to the inequitable political system and would
also create a popular demand for reform.

After Leandro Alem's suicide in 1892, Hipólito
Yrigoyen increasingly became the charismatic single
leader of the UCR. At the time, Yrigoyen exhibited the
two major traits that were to account both for his early
political success and his ultimate political failure.
He presented himself as "...a kind of apostle-harbinger

of democracy and the symbol of national reconcilia-
tion."[2]   At the same time, Yrigoyen was a tireless
organizer. He traveled throughout the country organizing local committees of the UCR everywhere:

> A meticulous organizer who created a disci-
> plined and loyal party structure through count-
> less individual interviews and small informal
> gatherings, he built an electoral machine which
> paralleled and often excelled that of the
> oligarchy.[3]

The strategy and tactics of the UCR and its leader
finally bore fruit after the electoral reform of 1912,
although certainly the long bitter time in the Argentine
political wilderness was utilized successfully.   By
1916, the party had broadened its appeal to the middle
class electorate. It had a national organization second
to none, and most importantly, perhaps, it possessed a
charismatic leader who radiated a mystical appeal to
Argentines desirous of change.   Thus, as the social and
economic fabric of the nation changed during the period
1890-1916, so finally did its politics. For the next
fourteen years, the UCR and Yrigoyen were faced with a
new set of problems: instead of acquiring power, they
now had to exercise it.

The six years of Yrigoyen's first presidency have
been subjected to varying interpretations.[4]   Several
facts stand out, however.   First, the UCR in the
presidency finally revealed its true colors. It was
not, as it had claimed, "radical" in the true sense of
the word, but instead was rather conservative in its
social outlook. Yrigoyen in the presidency was a great
deal less insistent upon change than was Yrigoyen in
opposition. Second, even if the Radicals had wished to
institute far-reaching social and economic changes, they
probably could not have done so. Yrigoyen had reached
the presidency as much through the good offices of the
conservatives as through his own efforts or those of his
party. Further, his electoral victory was exceedingly
slim. Even though he had won a majority of the popular
vote, his election was not assured until a small group
of dissident Radicals in Santa Fe eventually swallowed
their personal distaste for Yrigoyen and swung their
electoral votes his way. Further, the Radicals embarked
upon governing the country with a minority in the
Chamber of Deputies and only one Senate seat, which was
still elected by the Provincial assemblies. Control of
the Provinces was limited to Santa Fe, Cordoba, and
Entre Rios. The conservatives held sway in all the
rest. The electoral majority of the UCR, such as it
was, was also geographically unbalanced, pitting the
generally more liberal littoral area against the more
conservative interior. Yrigoyen, instead of trying to

expand the influence of the UCR into the interior, tried between 1916 and 1918 to steer a number of moderate reforms through the Congress. These reforms were generally aimed at benefitting the Radicals' supporters in the maritime regimes. Few of the proposals passed through the Congress, where the Senate was especially intransigent and dominated by the old conservative coalition. Yrigoyen's actions during the first two years of his administration succeeded only in alienating powerful political forces in the interior, while failing to provide any real gains for the government's supporters in and around Buenos Aires.

At the same time, the government tried to make good on some of its promises to the urban workers, supporting them in their strikes against the new industrialists. Once again, conservative interests proved too powerful for the Radicals, and the wave of strikes that followed Yrigoyen's assumption of the presidency led to a more powerful counter-reaction. Employers' organizations were formed as early as 1918, and para-military units such as the <u>Liga Patriotica Argentina</u> (Argentine Patriotic League) made their appearance. The League took measures against the strikers on several occasions. Union power was further diminished by the post-war economic stagnation after 1921.

Finally, the Radical administration encountered serious difficulties in its relations with the still-nascent middle class. Expansion of government services and spending were the key to increasing support from this group, but here again the initial policies of the Yrigoyen administration were nebulous at best, and after 1921 the expansionist policies of the government led to serious immediate, and ominously, longer-term financial difficulties.

In spite of what, in retrospect, were clear political and economic failures of the Yrigoyen administration, the appeal of the man himself was such that the elections scheduled for 1922 seemed to be a foregone conclusion. Yrigoyen was prohibited by the Constitution from succeeding himself, so he chose as the candidate of the UCR Marcelo T. Alvear, who had no personal following in the Party and who was widely assumed to be a puppet of the incumbent President. Alvear was elected with a much wider margin in both popular and electoral vote than Yrigoyen six years earlier. Although Yrigoyen retained control over the Party machinery, Alvear soon began to distance himself from the policies and the rhetoric of his mentor. At least until the end of the depression in 1925, Alvear proved to be much less committed to the middle class that made up much of the Party's rank and file, and to be more sympathetic to the needs of the more conservative landed and industrial elite. By 1923 the Party was completely divided, and in 1924 an attempt was made by followers of Alvear to wrest control of the party machinery from Yrigoyen. Although the attempt failed, the result was a split in the Party, with the new group, under the leadership of Alvear and Vicente Gallo, Minister of the Interior, calling themselves the Unión Cívica Radical Antipersonalista (Antipersonalist Radical Civic Union--UCRA). The bulk of the party faithful remained with Yrigoyen, however, and became known as Yrigoyenistas. For the rest of the decade, the most popular political movement in Argentina became Yrigoyenismo. The leader of this avowedly personalist movement began to rely more and more on his own brand of charisma and less and less on organization as the decade advanced.

By 1928, it had become apparent that Yrigoyen would again run for the presidency and that he would be elected overwhelmingly. The antipersonalista movement had largely fallen apart, as its leaders lacked both charisma and political acumen. Besides, Yrigoyen stood astride the Argentine political system like a colossus. He was at the height of his popularity which was due in perhaps equal parts to his own charismatic appeal to the rapidly expanding electorate and to the failure of both the conservative opposition and disaffected elements within the Radical movement to offer viable alternatives.

The elections of 1928 were a personal triumph for Hipolito Yrigoyen. This time he received an overwhelming victory in both popular and electoral votes, and the UCR, now securely under his domination, won control of the Chamber of Deputies. Only the Senate remained under conservative control and one of the new administration's avowed first goals was to change the method of electing Senators. Yrigoyen also again began making use of the intervention process, whereby the central government could replace elected officials at the Provincial level through the use of the military as a political tool. That this process, which Yrigoyen had also used extensively in his prior administration, was fraught with danger to the president himself seemed to be understood:

> The man who did most to undermine the non-involvement of the Argentine armed forces was Hipolito Yrigoyen....When he became President, he began to use the armed forces for internal political purposes....In this instance the effect of Yrigoyen's policy to intervene in provincial politics split the armed forces and was the beginning of fissures in them which have lasted down to the present day. The armed forces became part of the politcal process and a factor in decision-making whether they liked it or not. Some officers liked it; some did not. Whatever the balance of preference, the damage was done. The armed forces were in-

volved in politics because the President of the
Republic and their Commander-in-Chief had
willed it so.[5]

In the first year of the new Yrigoyen administration, it appeared that the new government might have a
chance of asserting its control over the country.
Although Yrigoyen had become a recluse, rarely appearing
in public, this only accentuated the aura of mysticism
that was part of his appeal to the masses. At the same
time, Argentina was enjoying an economic boom after
climbing out of the depression of 1921-1925, and the
government's redistributive policies could be implemented without injuring anyone; plus Yrigoyen could also
continue his strategy of employing vast patronage to
build political support.

It was at this point that the Great Depression
began to make its pressures felt on Argentina. Within a
few months, Yrigoyen's political strategy was in ruins,
and the government was attempting simply to survive
until the next election. In the March municipal
elections, "the opposition won victories in the capital
and in the provinces of Buenos Aires, Entre Rios, and
Cordoba, which gave the anti-Yrigoyenistas such strength
in Congress that they were able to block business by a
succession of legislative tricks."[6]

Demonstrations by students against the government
increased from March to September, and all the while the
President, old and perhaps senile, was unable to take
any decisive action to forestall the effects of the
depression. The inevitable occurred on September 6 when
elements of the armed forces marched from nearby army
and air force bases and deposed the Yrigoyen administration, thus bringing to an abrupt end a process which
began in the 1890s. The slow and painful process of
democratization and stabilization of Argentine politics
was done. From 1930 on, the armed forces, which had
increasingly been assuming an apolitical role in the
choice of national leaders, once again emerged as the
power brokers of the nation. The subsequent history of
Argentina, already alluded to, has been one of the
continuing breakdown and schism of the once proud UCR,
subsequently divided into two parties, the UCRP and the
UCRI. At the same time, the Peronist movement with its
openly class-based approach to politics, found itself
confronted by an implacable group of conservatives and
the armed forces. Any chance for compromise in Argentine politics was, perhaps, lost for the foreseeable
future during the decade of the 1920s. When one con-
siders the panoply of Argentine politics since 1930,
Hobbes and his war of all against all once again comes
to mind.

The great tragedy of Argentine politics, then, the
events and personalities that shape the unfortunate

state of affairs in that unhappy country in the 1980s, is not Peronism or the <u>gorilas</u> of the armed forces. All of these forces and more--the war of a succession of military governments against their own people, the <u>desparecidos</u>, the (now largely decimated) urban terrorist movement, but above all the political and social malaise that seems to affect most Argentines--have as their root cause the failure of an experiment in political party building that took place over fifty years ago. We shall, of course, never know definitely whether, if Yrigoyen had been able and willing to continue to build his party in the 1920s as he had in earlier times, events in 1930 might have turned out differently. It is, however, increasingly clear that a strong political party is a major obstacle to a military takeover in any country. If the UCR had been stronger in 1930, if Yrigoyen had not succumbed to the lure of <u>personalismo</u> and attempted one-man rule, the coup of 1930 might not have happened, and the subsequent political history of Argentina might have been much more felicitous than it has been. So once again, only this time in a negative vein, the political personality of the leader played a crucial role in determining not only the course of a political party, but the history of an entire nation as well. It is to that political personality that we now turn.[7]

The Leader

Hipólito Yrigoyen was born on July 12, 1852, in Buenos Aires. His father, Martin Yrigoyen Dodagaray, was a Basque immigrant, although none of the biographers seems to know when Martin emigrated to Argentina. Martin was, in the nature of the Basques, a hard worker. Although he had almost no education he soon went into the business of hauling people and goods from the ships arriving in the port to their final destination. By the time he was twenty-six, Martin had also been befriended by the Alem family, who by that time were operating a small dry-goods store on the outskirts of Buenos Aires. One of their daughters, Marcelina Antonia Alem Ponce, married Martin in 1847, and Hipolito was the first child of the union. The Alem family were native Argentines on both sides. Hipólito's grandfather, Don Leandro Antonio Alem, had been born in Buenos Aires in 1795, and had, for much of his adult life, been a minor official in the various regimes of the great <u>caudillo</u> of the early nineteenth century, Manuel Rosas.

This association with Rosas, and especially with a group of quasi-official thugs known popularly as "Mazorca," was to lead eventually to Don Leandro's execution by the Liberals under General Urquiza, who triumphed over Rosas in 1852, the same year Hipólito was born. Less than two years later, Hipólito's grandfather was killed by firing squad, and his body was left to hang in the Plaza de Concepcion for four hours after the execution. Thus was Hipolito Yrigoyen introduced to Argentine politics.

The period of youth and young adulthood was spent in comfortable financial circumstances, primarily under the roof of the Alem family. Martin gradually took over the family business, and managed to steer clear of politics. On the other hand, Hipolito's uncle, Leandro Alem was continually involved in the political struggles of the time, and was a major influence on the young Hipolito. This influence was strengthened when, at the age of ten, Hipólito was enrolled in the Colegio del America de Sud, a private secondary school for boys. Leandro Alem was a teacher in the school; teaching first and second years of philosophy. He popularized in his lessons some of his principal ideas, which his students assimilated. Hipólito remained at the Colegio until 1867, when he finished the secondary curriculum.

For the next ten years, Yrigoyen was employed in a variety of jobs, including lawyer's assistant, and local police official. He also entered the Law Faculty of the National University, but apparently, after successfully completing the first year of study, did not complete his degree. Instead, politics seemed to continually beckon, largely in the person of his uncle, Leandro Alem. Yrigoyen retained his post as police prefect while at the University, and on one occasion risked his life to protect his uncle from an armed group of political opponents. Finally, in 1878, Hipólito Yrigoyen was elected to the Chamber of Deputies. From that time on, Yrigoyen's life became a public one in an Argentina that was passing through a time of political troubles. The 1880s were a period of political turmoil in Argentina, and Hipolito Yrigoyen was, if not at the center of things, immersed in the politics of the times. One of the future president's major contributions was the founding, first, of several different political societies, and then in 1878, the Partido de Acción Nacional (Party of National Action--PAN), which was the forerunner of the UCR. From 1878 on, Hipólito Yrigoyen was a fervid politician. There was no distancing from the events and particularly the personalities of the time. All of the biographies make one point quite clear: Yrigoyen was more attached to the personalities than he was to either the issues or the institutions. The personality and thought of the leader were of utmost importance in determining Yrigoyen's political stance. This had, of course, always been true of his uncle, and Yrigoyen seemed to have learned his political lessons well. Perhaps because of his excessive emphasis upon personalities, Yrigoyen and his uncle began to drift apart politically and personally. Even at the meeting which celebrated the founding of the UCR, on September 1, 1889, Yrigoyen and his uncle, although once again on the same side politically, remained aloof from each other. The subsequent fight for control of the Party, and Alem's suicide, have never been fully explained except in terms of political personalities. Alem and Yrigoyen simply had different ideas about gaining political power. Alem, the older of the two, had suffered longer under unfriendly governments, and was less willing to wait for a peaceful evolution. Yrigoyen, on the other hand, refused to participate in several of Alem's revolutionary plots, much to the disgust of the uncle. As the UCR encountered increased vicissitudes during the early 1890s, the gulf between the uncle and nephew grew. Finally, on June 30, 1896, Leandro Alem committed suicide, leaving Hipólito Yrigoyen in effective command of the party they had both built. Later, of course, in the abortive revolution of 1905, Yrigoyen was to employ the same methods as his uncle.

Yrigoyen's private life during the period was barely existent. He lived for politics, while at the same time, exhibiting a negative attitude toward political office. Yrigoyen's personal physician has diagnosed him as a classic schizoid personality, and makes the point that schizoids display a negative personality. Yrigoyen always said "no" to appeals that he run for political office. Although he eventually would make the effort, there is little evidence that he derived any enjoyment, either from the contest or from the office, once it was achieved. His sense of mission was too enormous. He had to give the Argentines democratic government, and he had to do it himself. Unlike Betancourt in Venezuela, or Calles in Mexico, Yrigoyen had to achieve in a personal manner what others would allow institutions to do. The turbulence of his early years, the early introduction to passionate politics, based largely on personalismo, led to the conviction that he could be the great man for the Argentine nation. And a great man does not need institutions: he can perform by himself. In his early years, this tendency was perhaps masked by the exigencies of organizing an opposition to an entrenched oligarchy. From 1916 on, however, once in power, Yrigoyen resolved to do it all himself, with the disastrous results we have recorded.

An amazing parallel emerges here. James David Barber, in his study of presidential character in the United States, labels most of the conspicuous failures in American presidential history as "active-negative" personalities. By this, Barber means someone who is compelled to act in politics, but who derives no enjoyment from that actitivy. It is this combination, Barber argues, that leads to disaster in the presidency. Cross cultural parallels are, admittedly, dangerous, yet one cannot help but be struck by the similarity of political

temperament of Hipólito Yrigoyen and Richard Nixon.
Barber wrote his book in 1972, just after Nixon's
electoral triumph. Yet, on the basis of his analysis of
Nixons' political personality (active-negative), he pre-
dicted disaster for the incumbent president. Both Nixon
and Yrigoyen were driven, by forces deep in their childhood, to a sense of political mission. The missions
were not, of course, the same, but they were missions.
There is abundant evidence that neither Yrigoyen nor
Nixon derived any joy, or fun, or real satisfaction from
the pursuit of their missions. On the contrary, Barber
makes a convincing case that Nixon viewed the burdens of
the presidency in a negative way. There is also abundant evidence that Yrigoyen, too, viewed his political
activities in a negative light. A series of letters to
a defecting member of the UCR, published in 1909,
indicate, first, the sense of mission we have discussed,
but perhaps more importantly, a feeling that politics
was a burden he was forced to assume, and that he
derived no satisfaction from his political labors.
Yrigoyen, then, was in essence a loner. Forced in his
early political life to join and play the political
game, he did so. Once in power, however, he became ever
more reclusive and in the process wrecked his political
party and condemned the Argentine nation to over fifty
years of political hell.

Notes

1. Robert J. Shafer, A History of Latin America (Lexington, MA: D.C. Heath and Company, 1978), 376.
2. David Rock (ed.), Argentina In the Twentieth Century (Pittsburgh: University of Pittsburgh Press, 1975), 75.
3. James R. Scobie, Argentina: A City and a Nation (New York: Oxford University Press, 1964), 201.
4. Among the better books on Yrigoyen's political career and the politics of the times are: Jose Sivori, El Presidente Yrigoyen (Buenos Aires: Talleres Graficos Buenos Aires de la UCR del Pueblo, 1961); Gabriel del Mazo, Breve Historia del Radicalismo (Buenos Aires: Compania Editora y Distribuidora del Plata, 1964); Atilio Moro (ed.), Yrigoyen: Proceso de Su Gobierno (Buenos Aires: n.p., 1929); and Marvin Goldwert, Democracy, Militarism, and Nationalism In Argentina, 1930-1966 (Austin: University of Texas Press, 1972).
5. H. S. Fern, Argentina (New York: Frederick A. Praeger, 1969), 152.
6. Ibid., p. 158.
7. Perhaps the best study of Yrigoyen's political personality was written by his personal physician, Jose Landa, Hipólito Yrigoyen Visto Por Uno de Sus Medicos (Buenos Aires: Macland SRL, 1958). Other good books on Yrigoyen include: Gabriel del Mazo, El Pensamiento Escrito de Yrigoyen (Córdoba, Argentina: Union Civica Radical, 1976); Vida de Un Politico Argentino (Buenos Aires: Editoral Plus Ultra, 1976); Felix Luna, Yrigoyen (Buenos Aires, Editorial el Coloquio, 1975); Francisco Silva (ed.), Semblanzas de Yrigoyen (Buenos Aires: Talleres Graficas Argentino L. J. Rosso, 1928); Luis Sommi, Hipolito Yrigoyen, Su Vida y Su Epoca (Buenos Aires: Editorial Monteagudo, 1947); and Gabriel del Mazo, Politica Internacional del Presidente Yrigoyen (Montevideo: Consejo Departamental de Montevideo, 1960).

6
The Lion of Tarapacá

As all Chileans know, the "Lion of Tarapacá" was
Arturo Alessandri Palma, the dynamic, charismatic
politician who swept to political power in that country
in the 1920's, riding the wave of a burgeoning political
consciousness in the middle class and the Chilean
"rotos," the urban proletariat. Although he did not
finish his first term in office, resigning the presidency in late 1925 after a dispute with his defense
Minister, Alessandri was again elected to the Presidency
in 1932, and this time served his full six-year term
until 1938. Thus, Alessandri was the dominant political
figure in Chile during both the 1920s and 1930s. As
such, Arturo Alessandri had a great opportunity to build
political institutions for the Chilean future. That he
failed to do so contributed in ensuing years to a
deterioration and increasing fragmentation of the
Chilean political party system, the sharp polarization
of Chilean politics along ideological lines in the
1960s and 1970s, and the eventual military coup of 1973
and the subsequent harsh military dictatorship that
today governs that country. Alessandri, at least
nominally a member of the Radical Party, turned his back
on that great middle-class party coming out of the nineteenth century, and instead vacillated wildly between
left and right during his two terms in office, not
really identifying with or institutionalizing any
political party or group. Once again, as was the case
in other Latin American countries, the opportunity was
lost. The great political figure of the times had, for
reasons of his own political personality, chosen to
destroy rather than build, to rule through force of
personality rather than through institutions, and ultimately to severely damage his country's prospects for
future political peace and democratic politics.

The Setting

In the 1920s and 1930s, Chile was one of the most

94

modernized of the Latin American nations. The nation
had always considered itself apart from and superior to
much of the rest of Latin America, emphasizing in its
unofficial myths the European nature of its population,
the literacy of its people, and the orderly nature of
its political, social, and economic institutions. In
short, the Chileans felt a certain contempt for those
other Latin American nations (such as Peru) which were
less Europeanized, less literate, and less "developed"
than Chile.

At least some of these perceptions were supported
by the facts, while others were simply myths. Nevertheless, the myths continued to have a profound effect on
Chilean perceptions of the world, and on Chilean society
itself, as Chileans behaved as if their orderliness and
immunity from political turmoil and dictatorship were
somehow their birthright. At the same time, Chile was
in many ways a modern nation much earlier than many of
its Latin American neighbors. By the late 1930s,
Santiago, the capital, was a metropolis of over 800,000
people, and about 43 percent of the population of 4.7
million was urban. Literacy reached 51 percent in 1931,
which was high by Latin American standards of the time.
Chile had developed an industrial base during World War
I, and labor unions had developed even earlier than
that. By the 1930s, the unions played a major role in
Chilean politics, especially after the organization in
1931 of the Only Center of Chilean Workers (Central
Unico de Trabajadores Chilenos - CUTCh). Even so, control of the economic and political systems, and therefore of the society itself, remained largely in the
hands of a conservative group of owners of large estates
and a newer group of industrialists. The continued
ascendancy of this group was challenged during the two
decades of the 1920s and 1930s, but the masses were
never successful in changing or abolishing the entrenched elites. A major reason for this failure was the
restricted nature of the franchise: only adult literate
males were allowed to vote, which restricted the
potential electorate to less than one-quarter of the
total adult population. In addition, the opportunistic
nature of Alessandri himself contributed mightily to the
failure of the Radicals and others to successfully
challenge the continued hegemony of the old elites.
Although he originally came to power in 1920 on a
platform of ousting the elites from power, he never
actually implemented his campaign rhetoric, even during
his first years in office. By the time he was returned
to office in 1932, Alessandri had, like Grau in Cuba,
lost most if not all of his zeal for political change,
and cooperated intimately with the parties and groups on
the right. Both of Alessandri's terms in office were
marked by a continuing dispute between the legislature
and the president, and one outcome of his years in

office was a strengthening of the office of the presidency at the expense of the legislature. This institutionalization was especially marked during Alessandri's second term in the 1930s, when the Chilean army temporarily (as it turned out) retired from politics.

Perhaps Alessandri can be forgiven for viewing his main political task as that of taming a legislature that had effectively controlled the Chilean political process since 1891. He had originally run for President in 1920 on a platform of reform, not only in the social sphere but also of the parliamentary political system. Basically, Alessandri wanted to curb the power of the legislature and the elite at the same time, as these two institutions--one social and one political--worked hand in hand to perpetuate the status quo. The problem, by 1920, was that the status quo had become stagnation both politically and economically. Further, by 1920, as we have seen, the expanding social mobilization of the Chilean worker made such stagnation a major political liability for those who wished to perpetuate the ancien regime.

The year 1920 saw the crystallization of middle-class discontent in the candidacy of Arturo Alessandri over continued oligarchical rule and concomitant political inaction. In addition, Alessandri was supported by elements of the union movement not yet organized into socialist trade unions. Alessandri was the candidate of the Liberal Alliance, a coalition of the Radical and Democratic Parties. His conservative opponent, Luis Barros Borgoño, a landowning representative of the old elite, was the candidate of The National Union, an alliance of the Conservative and Liberal Parties. The election of 1920, viewed by many authors as a major turning point in Chilean politics, was extremely close, reflecting the real but waning power of the old coalition and the restricted nature of the electorate. Nevertheless, Alessandri won, and was duly inaugurated as President of the Republic. The next five years were ones of constant turmoil, as the reformist President battled his conservative opposition and later his own supporters in an attempt to push meaningful social and economic reforms. The continuing failure to achieve any breakthrough, plus the final spectacle in 1925, of the legislature (now under the control of the Liberals) preparing to vote itself a pay raise, brought the army back into Chilean politics after a hiatus of one hundred years. After a six month interregnum, Alessandri was back in office, but only for a short period of time. Once again, the Lion of Tarapacá proved unable to move events, and eventually turned over the reins of government to his Defense Minister late in 1925. The first attempt by Alessandri to move a nation had ended largely in failure. True, the new Constitution of 1925, which tilted the balance of political

power to the presidency, had been accepted; but beyond
that, the new middle-class groups who had been socially
mobilized during the first half of the twentieth century
had still to find a leader and a political party that
would represent their interests effectively in the
Chilean political system.

Why did this superbly gifted politician fail to
bring about changes desired by a majority of the voting
population? Part of the answer lies in describing the
changes in Chilean politics that had taken place in the
twentieth century, part lies in the political personality of Alessandri himself, and part lies in the
constellation of political forces existing at the time
in Chile.

The changing nature of Chilean society during the
early years of the twentieth century was at least
partially obscured by the existence of what has become
known as "The Parliamentary Republic" from 1891 to 1920.
The Republic in a sense represented a reaction to
earlier stages in Chilean politics, especially that from
1830 to 1861, in which presidential rule was autocratic
in nature. By the last half of the nineteenth century
this autocratic rule had evolved into a system whereby
presidents began to operate through the political
parties that had formed in the earlier period. The
three major parties--the Liberals, Conservative, and
Radical--began to have at least some influence on what
their candidates did once they assumed political office.
Then, in 1891, came the eight-month civil war which resulted in the parliamentary republic. The controversy
raged around the age-old question of just how much power
the president should possess. Violence between the
President and the Congress resulted in virtual destruction of executive preeminence. The parliamentary age,
lasting from 1891 to Alessandri's election in 1920, has
been characterized as "systematic disorder," by one
Chilean historian.[1] Presidents were barely able to
govern, and the Congress, with power in its hands, spent
its time corrupting the political process. Nevertheless, the period was one of relative political peace,
and this allowed the middle sectors, spurred on by the
growing industrialization and education, to gain some
political ground. As more middle-class males became
literate, they began to rail against the oligarchically
dominated Congress. Alessandri, with his charismatic
political style, and his vaguely populist platform,
provided the catalyst for this discontent. Even though
he was unable to complete his first term in office, the
1920's marked the end of the parliamentary period, and
also the end of complete dominance of Chilean politics
by the oligarchy. Henceforth the elite was to occupy a
minority position in electoral politics, even though
they continued to control the levers of power within the
government.

   In addition to the destruction of the parliamentary
regime, the years from 1920 to 1938 also brought about
some other real changes in the Chilean political system.
The military, which virtually ruled the country from
Alessandri's resignation in 1925 to his reelection in
1932, actually subjected the country to more rapid and
fundamental change than had any of the preceding
civilian administrations, including that of Alessandri.
Carlos Ibanez, the leading figure in the government of
the period, was perhaps the first Latin American practi-
tioner of what has become known as the "modernizing
authoritarian" form of government, now seen in Brazil
and other countries. Ibanez spent considerable sums of
money on education, urban services, transportation, and
other governmental programs aimed at rationalizing and
modernizing the Chilean economy. At the same time, his
regime clamped down on organized labor and other opponents, throwing them in jail when necessary, and in
general violating the rights guaranteed by the Constitution of 1925. Ibanez finally resigned under pressure in
1931, and for the next year Chile experienced a series
of unstable governments, reminiscent of the 1924-1927
period.
   Alessandri's return to the presidency in 1932 was
marked by initial jubilation on the part of the middle-
class groups which had supported him in 1920.   The
jubilation was, however, short-lived, as it soon became
apparent that the revolutionary of the 1920s had become
the defender of the status quo in the 1930s.   Actually,
Alessandri was elected this time with the support from
center groups, with his leftist support going to
Marmaduke Grove, a colleague of Ibanez in the army and
by this time an avowed socialist. The second Alessandri
regime was, in essence, a pause in the reformist rhythm
generated by Alessandri and the army during the 1920s,
as Alessandri increasingly allied himself with the
conservative elements within the Radical Party and with
the rightist Conservative and Liberal parties.
Alessandri's actions led to a split within the Radical
party, which reflected to a degree the internal divisions of the Party. A significant portion of the
Radicals made the leap to a National Front coalition
with the Communists and Socialists, declaring in 1936
that the Party recognized "the class struggle" and
"proletarian vindication." The Front immediately scored
an electoral success in the 1937 congressional elections, securing over 40 percent of the vote. Then, in
the 1938 presidential elections, the Front candidate,
Radical Pedro Aguirre Cerda, won the presidency with
50.6 percent of the vote. Political mobilization and
activism were again on the upswing, and the left had
become, rather suddenly, a major force in Chilean
politics, as the former great middle-class party--the
Radicals--had made common cause with the parties of the

left. Alessandri, unable to run for immediate re-election and now rejected by the party he had ignored in earlier years, was left to become in later years a symbol of the political changes in Chile during the 1920s and 1930s. The sudden emergence of the left in the new political alliance was to affect every subsequent political campaign in Chile, although its full effect would not be felt for another thirty years. Since the 1930s, the Radical Party has wandered across the Chilean political landscape, first allying itself with the left (1938, 1942, 1946), then with the right (1970), while at times preferring to go it alone (1952, 1958, 1964). During this period, the percentage of the vote garnered by Radical candidates, either alone or in coalition, steadily declined, as this once-great party of the Chilean middle class lost its hold on the Chilean electorate, setting the stage for the demise of Chilean democracy in 1973.

The Leader

Thousands of pages and hundreds of leaflets have been published about his life, and while this bibliography lengthens the task of contemporary and future historians to give to this personality his own character, to discover the multiform ramifications of his mind or to place the definitive and impartial seal of history on his life becomes ever more difficult.[2]

Arturo Alessandri is one of those personalities Chile will never forget; his name belongs to the nation's history; and although the hatred of a few still works against his memory, the constructive work done by the caudillo and statesman becomes more important every day. In a short time no one will dispute the place that he has gained next to Bernardo O'Higgins, Diego Portales, Manuel Montt, and Jose Manuel Balmaceda.[3]

Throughout his stormy existence, his work as agitator and destroyer of institutions predominates...Studied with serenity, his activity doesn't go beyond that of an opportunistic politician, quick to capture the predominant ideological currents, without being animated by any grand, transcendent, ennobling idea.[4]

The above are but a small sampling of the writings on the life and works of Arturo Alessandri Palma, the Lion of Tarapacá. To some, the savior of the Chilean nation; to others, one who destroyed the precious insti-

tutions that held Chilean society together. One part of
the quotations is true, however, and beyond dispute:
Arturo Alessandri is one of those personalities Chile
will never forget.[5]

Arturo Alessandri Palma was born on December 20,
1868, in the town of Longaví, in North-Central Chile.
His paternal grandfather, Pedro Alessandri, emigrated to
Chile from Argentina in 1823, having visited the country
first in 1821 as a member of a traveling circus. Pedro
had been born in Italy, and had come to Argentina some
years earlier. He was twenty-seven years old when he
arrived in Santiago, and by the time his only son Pedro
was born in 1838, the elder Pedro had achieved some
position and a small fortune as a businessman in
Valparaiso. On his death in 1827, the grandfather left
a considerable fortune to his son, who used the money
primarily to establish himself as a farmer and landowner. By the time his third son Arturo was born, Pedro
had moved from Valaparaiso to the finca Longavi, near
the town of Linares. Arturo's youth was spent as a
member of the expanding Chilean bourgeoisie. As such,
Arturo enjoyed most comforts and many of the luxuries
offered in the 19th century Chile. In 1880, at the age
of twelve, Arturo was sent to a Colegio of the
Franciscan Fathers in Santiago, to pursue his studies
toward the bachillerato degree. The Colegio was known
as a training ground for the sons of the conservative
establishment in Chile, and Arturo spent seven years
there, receiving his bachillerato early in 1888. From
the Colegio, armed with his bachillerato, Arturo began
pursuing a law education, while at the same time gaining
employment as an assistant in the National Library in
Santiago. The Revolution of 1891 interrupted young
Alessandri's studies only temporarily, as he wrote
approvingly of the Revolution and its attempt to oust
the "dictator" Balmaceda. Once the Revolution had
achieved its end, and Balmaceda had been ousted,
Alessandri returned to the study of law, receiving his
title of lawyer on January 6, 1893. Shortly after, he
renounced his position with the National Library, and
began practicing as an attorney. The young lawyer
married Rosa Esther Rodriquez, granddaughter of Bernardo
O'Higgins, daughter of the Minister of Finance, and a
member in good standing of Chilean society.
Alessandri's career was on the upswing. He participated
in the presidential campaign of 1896, having been named
a deputy to the convention that nominated Federico
Errazuriz as candidate of the coalition of the Liberal
and National parties. Errazuriz was elected President
in an election ultimately decided by the Congress, while
Alessandri began his political career as a member of the
Chamber of Deputies. He remained as Deputy from the
Province of Curico until his election as Senator from
the Province of Tarapacá in 1915. By now Alessandri was

the candidate of the Radical Party, having moved left-ward in his political journey of the last nineteen years. Successful in the election, Alessandri immediately began to criticize the parliamentary regime dominated by the oligarchy. By 1920 his oratory had made him the leading candidate of the parties of the center-left in Chilean politics. The National Alliance was composed of the National Party, the Democratic Party, and the left wing of the Radical Party (to which Alessandri nominally belonged). The election was hard-fought and close, with the final result being decided by a "Tribunal of Honor," agreed to beforehand. Alessandri was declared the winner, and swept into office on a wave of popular enthusiasm.

The next five years were among the most frenetic in Chilean political history, as Alessandri tried to wrest power from the old guard while at the same time transforming the Chilean political system from one dominated by parliament to one of presidential supremacy. Ultimately, the President failed in his first task, but largely succeeded in his second, although it eventually took the Chilean army to complete the task of vesting political power increasingly in the hands of the middle class.

By 1932, when Alessandri again was vaulted to power, largely by the Radical Party, he had evidently resolved to come to terms with a still vital oligarchy and a military that had shown itself capable of inter-vening in politics if things did not go its way. For the next six years, "Alessandri, elected by the Left, governed with the Right."[6] This time, he finished his term in office, due in large part to his strategy of turning his back on those who were responsible for his election. By the time Alessandri left office in 1938, the Radical Party had lost its chance to become the controling factor in Chilean politics. Only if the Party and Alessandri had formed a close union, only if Alessandri had concentrated on identifying himself with the Party (and vice versa) could the Radicals have achieved the position of supremacy they perhaps merited in Chilean politics. For the Radical Party was the dominant multi-class party in Chile at the time. It was the best-organized, one of the best financed, and with Alessandri its leader, would have been able to appeal to practically all segments of the Chilean voting public.

However, this was not to be. Alessandri, never a committed party man, had changed parties as he changed ideological and political convictions. In a sense, Alessandri was a child of his political times; for he grew up in a Chile marked by the byzantine political alliances of the Parliamentary era, when leaders and parties coalesced and split with bewildering frequency. Then, of course, came the question of charisma. Alessandri's entire political career, from 1898 to his

death in 1950 (when he was President of the Chilean
Senate, having been elected as a candidate of the
Liberal Party) was upwardly mobile. He never needed an
organization to further his political ambitions. Unlike
Calles or Trujillo, he could achieve his political ends
through force of personality alone. In fact, not only
his political career, but Alessandri's whole life was
upwardly mobile. Born to a wealthy family, marrying
well, law school, successful practice, a Deputy at age
twenty-nine, elected Senator on his first try against
formidable odds, then President against the wishes of an
entrenched oligarchy--what more could a person want out
of life, and why bother with organizational work, which
would be boring compared to the heady success of
personal political and personal victories?

One of Alessandri's biographers labels him an
"agitator and destroyer." Others disagree, and in fact
the biographer in question refers not to political
parties but the ancien regime put permanently out to
pasture in 1920. But the fact is that Alessandri was a
destroyer: he destroyed, perhaps unintentionally, the
strongest political party in Chile at the time, and the
one party that might have become the balance wheel of
Chilean politics for decades to come. The use of the
word "agitator" is also instructive, as this was the
term used by Harold Lasswell in his bestiary of
political types presented in 1930. The agitator,
according to Lasswell is so busy with change and with
creating and entering into controversy, that he has no
time to build. This, it appears, was the legacy of
Arturo Alessandri Palma in Chile. When the pressures
began to mount in the early 1970s, the political party
that had supported Alessandri but which had not received
support in return--the Radicals--could play but a minor
role in the sad events that led to the cruel military
dictatorship that has ground Chile under its heel since
1973.

Notes

1. Francisco Frias, Manual de Historia de Chile
(Santiago de Chile: Editorial Nascimiento, 1975), 42.
2. Virgilio Figueroa, Diccionario Historico y
Biografico de Chile (Nendeln, Lichtenstein: Kraus-
Thomson Organization, 1974), 355.
3. Fidel Arañeda Bravo, Arturo Alessandri Palma
(Santiago, Chile: Editorial Nascimiento, 1979), 9.
4. Ricardo Donoso, Alessandri: Agitador y
Demoledor (Mexico: Fondo de la Cultura Economica,
1954), 9.
5. Other biographies of Alessandri include:
Augusto Iglesias, Alessandri: Una Etapa de la Democracia en America (Santiago, Chile: Instituto Chileno
de Estudios Humanisticos, 1979); plus two books by
Alessandri himself: El Presidente Alessandri A Traves
de Sus Discursos y Actuacion Politica (Santiago de
Chile: Biblioteca Americana, 1926); and Recuerdos de
Gobierno (Santiago, Chile, Editorial Nascimiento, 1967),
3 vol's.
6. Claudio Orrego et al, 7 Ensayos Sobre Arturo
Alessandri Palma (Santiago de Chile: Instituto Chileno
de Estudios Humanisticos, 1979), 394.

7
Ramón Grau San Martín
and the Cuban Revolution

The Cuban revolution of Fidel Castro has captured the imagination of the media and the public alike as has no other twentieth century event in Latin America. Since Castro's triumph in 1959, reams of material have poured out of the printing presses assessing the reasons for the triumph in one of the richest countries in Latin America (and, as we are continually reminded, one only ninety miles from home) of a Marxist-Leninist revolution inimical to our ideals and our interests. Out of all this material, only a few voices have been raised linking the events of an earlier era to the events in Cuba of the 1950s and after. These few voices are, however authoritative. Hugh Thomas in his massive study of Cuban history states that the events of 1959 were a direct consequence of the events of 1933.[1] Luis Aguilar, in his masterful examination of the events of that year, states:

> One fact as least appears certain: the Cuban society that Castro found in 1959 was basically forged by the forces that emerged and grew out of the revolutionary episode of 1933.[2]

The lesson is clear: in order to understand Cuba today--the reasons for the success of the Revolution of 1959, the popular attitudes toward democratic government, the attitudes of the Cubans toward the United States--we must go back in history to the early 1930s. If we do not do this, we cannot understand what happened in more recent times: all of the socio-political explanations of the forces at work in Cuba in the 1950s that brought Castro to power ultimately fail in their explanatory power if the political history of the 1930s is ignored. Cuba, then, is the leading proof of the major thesis of this book: political events of the 1920s and 1930s affected and continue to affect the political process, not only of Cuba, but of all Latin American countries; and we must understand those events if we are to understand today's political events.

Cuba in 1933 lay under the boot of yet another in a line of venal and brutal dictators going back to the island's independence from Spain in 1898. Interspersed with these dictators had been a series of dictatorships of another sort: open and unenlightened intervention by the United States, under the provisions of the infamous Platt Amendment.[3] Cuba in 1933 was, in common with other nations of the world, also in the throes of the world depression. Gustavo Machado, the current dictator, had been in power since his election as President in 1924. The elections, which Machado had won overwhelmingly on a nationalist platform, had been basically honest, and many Cubans were beginning to feel that at last a new day had dawned for the Republic. Such was not to be the case, however. Machado was possessed by an almost insatiable desire for power, and this desire began to assert itself at about the mid-point of his supposed four-year term. Additionally, "The impact of Machado's personality, the lack of true leadership in the political parties, and the noxious tendency to follow dogmatic individuals were felt in Cuban politics from the very beginning of the Republic."[4] There was, in effect, no political infra-structure to oppose the would-be demagogue. Political parties in Cuba in the 1920s were weak: they were mainly collections of ambitious politicians trying to hitch their wagon to the star of the leader who would be successful. Parties were collections of people cele-brating the cult of personalismo rather than on their way to becoming institutionalized organizations. Machado himself disdained party development and instead relied on his own charisma to further his rule. In the opposi-tion to Machado, only one organized group stood out: the so-called ABC. The name developed from the character of the organization in 1931: it was an organ-ization divided into cells, with eight members of Cell A each commanding subordinate cells (B,C, etc). Thus the name ABC. The ABC was organized; however, the leader-ship decided to pursue a two-pronged strategy to rid Cuba of Machado. Open opposition would be pursued when possible, but terrorist activities would also be employed. Given the nature of the situation, terrorism became increasingly the major method of opposition used by the ABC. In spite of its terrorist activities, the ABC was the one of a few programmatic oppositionist groups in Cuba. Its Manifesto, issued in 1932, was one of the most far-reaching programs for the reform of Cuban politics of the times. While stressing its anti-communism, the organization stressed the need for a basic restructuring of both the Cuban economy and Cuban society.

The other organized and non-personalist opposition group was the Directorio Estudiantil (Student

Directorate) of the National University in Havana.
Although beset by ideological schisms, primarily between
the Marxists and non-Marxists, the Directorate managed
to present a program designed to appeal to those who
wished to reform Cuban politics and society. The
Directorate was, as the name implies, composed primarily
of university students, plus a large number of professors who supported their political aims.

Despite the machinations of both the ABC and the
Student Directorate, the coup de grace to the Machado
regime came from an unlikely source: the non-
commissioned officers in the Cuban army, led by Sergeant
Major Fulgencio Batista. Machado himself, under heavy
pressure from U.S. Ambassador Sumner Welles to resign,
did so on August 12, 1933, and was replaced the next day
by Carlos Manuel de Céspedes who was inaugurated as
provisional President. Céspedes was a colorless
politician with no following in the country save Welles,
and he had been installed almost at the direction of the
Ambassador. The country by this time, however, was
almost totally in a state of anarchy, with the strikes
that had contributed to the toppling of Machado continuing. In addition, in Havana people were taking
personal vengeance against the agents of the former
Machado regime, with lynchings in the streets on some
occasions. On August 24, the Student Directorate issued
its Manifesto, condemning the hated Machado regime, U.S.
intervention, and the provisional government. The
government was a "severe denunciation of the provisional
government, the ABC, and the whole political power
structure."[5] Two days later came the Sergeants' coup
led by Batista, followed by the installation of the
famous "Pentarchy" or provisional government of five.
The National Palace was open to anyone who wished to
join the discussions on the future of the Republic.
Students, enlisted army men, and some younger members of
the ABC dominated the meetings, along with the
Pentarchy. Chief among the members of the Pentarchy was
a forty-six year old medical doctor and Professor of
Medicine at the University, Dr. Ramón Grau San Martín.

For the next five days the Pentarchy tried to
govern a country in the grip of revolutionary turmoil.
It soon became apparent, however, that the most the five
could do was to disagree on the proper course of action.
One of the few actions taken during the five days was to
name former Sergeant Batista as Chief of Staff of the
Army, a move that prompted the resignation of Porfirio
Franca, the most popular member of the Pentarchy.
Batista's nomination was agreed to less than enthusi-
astically by at least two other members of the ruling
junta, but the nomination finally carried. Quite
probably, the situation in the streets made it impera-
tive that Batista be named to the post. The soldiers
patrolling were, for the most part, loyal to him, and it

was becoming increasingly clear that Batista was no ordinary sergeant, but that he harbored political ambitions. Further, the political situation was so volatile that the Pentarchy could not know from one day to the next from what quarter its political support might emanate, or what group might suddenly oppose the new and fragile government. In reality, the revolution relied for its support on an unlikely coalition of students and soldiers, and this coalition was volatile, to say the least.

By September 9, there was increasing evidence that the Pentarchy and Batista were no longer on good terms. Soldiers had been acting without orders from anyone but Batista, and Batista had gone to the deposed president Cespedes to indicate that he, Batista, would support him for president once again if Cespedes would confirm him as Army Chief of Staff. On the evening of the 9th, beset by an inability to act to control the situation, by increasing opposition from a variety of sectors, and by internal dissension, the Pentarchy was informed by the students that Grau San Martín should be named President. Grau thereupon became President of Cuba by acclamation.

As things turned out, Grau had only four months to build a political coalition that would withstand the challenges it might face from both the right and left. In this sense, the situation in Cuba was unlike those in Mexico, the Dominican Republic, Venezuela, and Argentina, in which the leader had the luxury of time in which to build a political organization. In reality, the situation of Grau in Cuba in 1933 placed him much closer to the "actor dispensable" end of Greenstein's continuum than, say, Calles in Mexico. Nevertheless, Grau did have some time, and he did not use it effectively.

To be sure, the new government faced the same problems as did the old Pentarchy. Sumner Welles, the U.S. Ambassador, was implacably opposed to "the communistic element" which had taken over the country. Moreover, he personally disliked Grau, and was able to keep the U.S. government from recognizing the new government, a decision that by itself had always been enough to sound the death-knell for any new government on the island. His successor, Jefferson Caffery, who arrived in Cuba on December 8 as Roosevelt's special representative instead of Ambassador, was also implacably opposed to a continuation of the Grau government.[6] As Welles himself stated, "no government here can survive for a protracted period without recognition by the U.S."[7] The ABC, partially discredited by the events of the year, and bitterly opposed by the Grau administration, published its own denunciation of the new order on September 11. The communists, who had been quiet during the events up to September, now staged a

demonstration in which they denounced the Grau government and labeled it a lackey of the Americans. Most
ominously, discipline in the army was slipping, and
Batista knew it. The culmination of this deterioration
was yet another army revolt in early November, in which
elements disaffected from Batista tried to take charge
of several army camps. The revolt was put down with
unbridled ferocity by Batista and his men, but it demonstrated to him that he could not wait forever to make
his move. Inaction was eroding his support in the armed
forces.

At the same time, the new government was, in many
ways, its own worst enemy. Grau proved to be an
indecisive political leader, and almost completely under
the spell of the Student Directorate. Even though the
new government began issuing a flood of decrees, many of
which embodied the major promises of the revolution
(and, incidentally, provided the basis for many of the
decrees issued by the 26 of July movement after their
triumph in 1959), the exact status of Grau in all this
was perhaps best outlined by Ruby Hart Phillips, the New
York Times correspondent in Havana:

> Amid the screams of urchins who demand (one) to
> (be careful of the machine)...knowing I can't
> possibly get near the elevator, I take the
> stairs and on the second floor find myself in
> another crowd. Finally I arrive at the Cabinet
> room where President Grau receives everyone.
> It is a long narrow table. The President sits
> at the head of the table surrounded by the
> Directorate...A couple of hours later, I had
> progressed several places toward the head of
> the table where Grau is now totally obscured
> from my view by excited, youthful nation-
> savers. Eventually, I get within striking
> distance and, finding that a woman's voice will
> make itself distinct, I ask a question. The
> President replies, looking right at me but not
> in answer to my questions. No one around the
> President pays the slightest attention to
> him.[8]

Other analyses of the period highlight the apparent
differences among Grau, his young minister of Interior
Antonio Guiteras, and Batista as the major cause of the
downfall of the revolutionary government.[9] In retrospect, of course, the eventual outcome was probably
inevitable: the Grau government (if it can be called
that) was facing a conglomeration of forces, both exter-
nal and internal working for its downfall. Finally, in
early January, 1934, almost four months to the day after
the Sergeants' revolt had toppled the Cespedes government, Batista acted. The counter-revolution when it

came was bloodless: Batista merely convinced the mob in
the National Palace that Grau would have to go. Grau
himself appeared to be willing to relinquish power. So,
on January 15, 1934, Grau resigned in favor of Carlos
Hevia, an old-line politician put forward by Batista.
The revolution of 1933 was over.

For the next twenty-six years, Cuban politics had
one major theme: you were either for Batista or you
were against him. Even though the Auténticos and Grau
himself had another chance at governing from 1944 to
1952, Batista remained behind the scenes, waiting for
the revolutionaries of 1933 to fail again. And fail
they did:

> Dr. Ramón Grau San Martín was now almost sixty
> years old. He embodied in 1944 the hopes of
> hundreds of thousands of Cubans who wanted a
> secure future for themselves and their child-
> ren, a serious and socially conscious govern-
> ment free from corruption, and one which was
> essentially, in some clear if undefined and
> 'Martian' way, Cuban. He betrayed these hopes
> utterly. The trust which the people of Cuba
> had in him was wasted in a revel of corrupt
> government which rivaled the era of Zayas and
> exceeded that of Batista. Already a rich man
> due to an extensive private practice and the
> fortune which he inherited from his father...,
> Grau turned his presidency into an orgy of
> theft, ill-disguised by emotional nationalistic
> speeches. He did more than any other single
> man to kill the hope of democratic practice in
> Cuba.[10]

The problem with corruption under the second Grau
administration, which lasted from 1944 to 1948, was that
it was so blatant, with the proceeds accruing to a small
number of Grau's friends. In other words, there was no
political machine to keep graft within bounds and to
distribute the graft more widely among deserving members
of the machine. The contrast with Mexico at about the
same time could not be more stark. The political
machine created by Calles and strengthened by succeeding
Presidents, especially Cardenas, had succeeded by the
1940's in completely dominating the political process in
Mexico. At the same time, graft became institutionalized as did the PRI. However, the machine knew, almost
instinctively, how much graft was enough, or what the
people would stand for. Further, the machine made sure
that graft was widely enough distributed so that a large
number of would-be critics of the regime would be bought
off, or co-opted, to use a word now almost synonymous
with Mexican politics. In Cuba, on the other hand,
graft and corruption were a purely personal matter, in

the hands of Grau and his sycophants at court. Grau's successor, Carlos Prio Socarras, also an Auténtico, continued and even increased the amount of graft and corruption in the only two democratic administrations the Cubans had had since the 1920s. Small wonder that, by 1952, democracy was in bad odor in Havana. When the second Batista coup came, in 1952, most Cubans either breathed a sigh of relief or at the least did not oppose the abrupt end of democratic government on that unhappy island.

By 1952, the Auténticos were finished as a political party. They had never achieved a true sense of organization, they had never been able to convincingly present themselves as a viable alternative to dictatorship, and with their demise went the last chance for any alternative to dictatorship of the right or the left. A year later, a young university student named Fidel Castro Ruz led an attack on the Moncada army barracks near Santiago, and Cuban politics entered a new stage of left-right confrontation, in which the gap between left and right had widened greatly.

The Leader

Any history of the Auténtico movement from its inception in 1933 until its practical demise in 1952 must inevitably take into account the political personality of its leader during all those years. When he first ascended to power in 1933, Dr. Ramón Grau San Martín was unknown outside a small circle in the National University, where he taught medicine; Grau at the time was in his mid-forties and had been exiled from Cuba during the last half of the Machado regime because of his intemperate denunciations of Machado at the University. Grau had been born into an upper-class Cuban family (his father was a tobacco wholesaler) and spent his early years attending fashionable private schools in the Vedado section of Havana. At the time, the Vedado was the most fashionable area of the city, and even in the 1950s, after Miramar had become the haven for the nouveau riche as well as the sugar aristocracy, Vedado remained the preserve of many of the older, well-established elite. By the time he was propelled into politics in 1933, Grau had created a solid reputation as an excellent doctor to much of Havana society, as well as one of the best-liked professors at the University of Havana. Interestingly, unlike other Latin American political leaders of the time, there does not appear a full-length biography of Grau; we must make do with bits and pieces from different authors in order to fit together the puzzle of his character.[11]

Certainly one aspect of Grau's character was his personal bravery. He first came to national attention in 1928, when the Machado police entered the University, and Grau (among others) refused to continue teaching surrounded by soldiers. For his act of defiance he was thrown into the penitentiary on the Isle of Pines, traditionally a place of repose for those who opposed the government. From the Isle of Pines, Grau was eventually allowed to move into exile in Miami, where he became a leader in the somewhat fragmented exile movement in that city (then as today a place where exile movements attempted to organize against the dictator of the moment). Grau also was possessed of a large degree of personal charisma. His speeches, which tended to be long and somewhat rambling, invariably stirred deep emotions among his listeners. At his inauguration as President on September 10, instead of taking the oath inside the National Palace as had been prescribed, Grau proceeded to the balcony, "where amid the cheers of the multitude he swore to fulfill the program of the Revolution."[12]

Grau also appeared, at least in the early days of the 1930s, to be decisive. The one hundred twenty days of his government were marked by a sincere attempt to at least begin the implementation of the goals of the Revolution. As Grau himself stated, the goals of the Revolution were nationalism, non-Marxist socialism, and anti-imperialism. In the first few days of his government, decrees were issued abrogating the hated Platt Amendment, which had given the United States the right to intervene unilaterally in Cuban affairs. In addition, a Department of Labor was created for the first time in Cuban history, the University of Havana was given autonomy, importation of cheap labor from Haiti and Jamaica was forbidden, and a decree established an eight-hour day for all workers. Perhaps he was moving too fast, but he was driven by the students, especially Guiteras, to make the revolution a reality within a short time. "Grau was slightly over six feet tall, thin, and anemic looking. A bachelor, he devoted most of his time to his practice and his students."[13] It was, perhaps, this close association with (some might say slavish association) the students that eventually caused Grau's downfall in 1933. Congenitally, Grau was an idealist, and the idealistic streak among his students was echoed in the new President and leader of the Auténticos. The idealism was reflected both in Grau's speeches and in the torrent of decrees that issued from the Palace during the four months of his regime. However, all this activity and talking left too little time for coalition and institution-building. The truth is that by January, 1934, the Auténticos were no nearer any real organization as a mass-based political party than they had been at the beginning of 1933, when they first organized.

The history of the Auténticos and of Grau himself

112

during the ten year period from Batista's coup in early
1934 to Grau's triumphant return as President in 1944
has not been told with any clarity. Certainly, this was
a period, much like that suffered by the Adecos of
Venezuela between their ouster in 1946 and their return
in 1958, which could have been a fruitful one for party
organization. Instead, it appears to have been largely
frittered away in attempts to dislodge Batista through
strikes and other political machinations, all of which
failed. Little of no attempt was made, by Grau or
others, at political party institutionalization. In the
jargon of political science:

> From the early 1930s through the late 1950s the
> Cuban political system successfully separated
> the politics of government from the politics of
> incumbency. Interest-group access to govern-
> ment was direct and institutionalized.
> Competition for incumbency remained in a 'pure'
> political arena. Cleavages linked to the
> society and economy were reflected directly in
> government rather than through the political
> party system....Political competition among
> individuals and parties was characterized both
> by distance from cleavages and by vola-
> tility.[14]

What is being stated here is that Grau and others
failed to take advantage of their time in exile to build
a true political organization. From his exile in Mexico
Grau did attempt to build some political bridges, but
most of his time was spent denouncing Batista and planning ways to re-acquire power in Cuba. Here too, the
idealistic, charismatic, almost mystical nature of
Grau's political personality seemed to stand in the way
of embarking on the patient, long-term organizational
work necessary to construct a political machine capable
of withstanding the shocks that first Batista and later
Castro were capable of administering. What Grau lacked
in organizational skill and interest, Antonio Guiterras
perhaps had. We shall never know, however, as Guiteas
was one of the first casualties of the Batista years:
he was killed by elements of Batista's army in a fire
fight in March, 1935.

The verdict on Grau is not unanimously harsh.
Aguilar finds him to be the epitome of Cuban nationalism:

> Under an outward appearance of very gentle
> manners Ramón Grau San Martín hid a strong
> character and the capacity to make decisions
> and keep them. He also had a dramatic instinct
> for the right gesture, a political conscious-
> ness of being on stage...A distinguished

physician and university professor, Grau seems
to have had few definite political convictions,
but once he sided with the students and became
a revolutionary leader he fought bravely--and
with considerable opportunism--to keep that
public image.[15]

Hugh Thomas is somewhat less laudatory, but nevertheless, gives the early Grau rather high marks:

He was unknown to more than a small circle. He
seemed to be a new man, respectable and
scholarly, with some knowledge of the world derived from an extensive medical practice in
Havana. He looked nervous and emotional, but
at that time that was attributed to his excessive honesty and dedication to the cause of
authentic revolution. Effeminate in looks yet
lecherous, seemingly earnest but a brilliant
and malicious wit, Grau San Martin appeared indecisive and weak while (he) was actually ruthless, cunning, and brave.[16]

Ramon Eduardo Ruiz is not as kind to Grau:

As chief executive he proved weak, procras-
tinating on key decisions or leaving them to
others, while his administrative ability was
virtually nil. He was a neophyte in the world
of practical politics; questions of ideology
bored him--he claimed his regime was
'apolitical.' He wanted, nonetheless, social
justice for his people, but his romantic faith
was not reciprocated by Cubans, who could not
understand him....Grau captured the presidency
with the aid of the students; once in office,
however, they overwhelmed his administration
and complicated the task of government, their
idealism and enthusiasm proving poor
substitutes for experience.[17]

In terms of party institutionalization, Grau
committed one further sin. The vast amount of corruption in his government (1944-1948) and that of Carlos
Prio Socarras (1948-1952) led eventually to a schism
within the Auténticos. A group of disenchanted younger
members of the party founded a dissident wing in 1947
and called themselves the Ortodoxos, implying they were
the real heirs of the Revolution of 1933. The schism,
while regarded as important at the time, in reality
merely provided the coup de grace to a political party
that had never really been organized. In time, the
Ortodoxos, like the party they grew out of, also began
quarreling among themselves, and splinter movement

114

after splinter movement began to appear, each attached
to the political personality of the moment.

Epilogue

It should be by now obvious that Cuban politics
from 1933 to 1959 presented a series of lost opportunities for all the players. The United States might, if
it and its representatives in Havana had been more
farsighted in 1933, have avoided the necessity of coming
to grips with a Marxist-Leninist revolution on the
island after 1959. Fulgencio Batista, if he had been
less sanguinary in his rule and had been better able to
control some of the thugs and sadists that surrounded
him, especially after 1952, might have retained at least
a modicum of popular support in Cuba, plus the continued
support of the United States government. As it was, he
lost both power bases largely because he could not or
would not stop the tortures and killings that marked the
later years of his regime. Certainly, the greatest lost
opportunity belonged to Grau San Martín and the
Auténicos. Beginning in 1933 with the nationalist anti-
imperialist revolution of that year, the Auténticos
represented the very real yearnings and aspirations of
the rapidly growing Cuban middle class, as well as
ordinary Cubans of all walks of life. What the Cuban
people wanted was a government that was not too corrupt,
that would stand up to the United States, and that would
bring a modicum of stability and social justice to an
island nation that had never had either of these in any
great quantity. The tragedy is that this is what Grau
and the Auténticos wanted also, but they were unable to
deliver on their promises to the Cuban people. Instead
of controlling events and the larger than life personalities of Batista and Castro as they appeared on the
Cuban stage, the Auténticos lapsed into puerile
quarreling among themselves and, when they obtained
power, used it only as a means to seek personal
aggrandizement. While Grau could not totally control
the outcome of events in 1933, the lost opportunities of
the subsequent years in exile and the years in power
from 1944 to 1952 were more amenable to the maneuverings
of an institutionalized political party. Once again,
the analogy with events in Venezuela is painful. By the
time Acción Democrática was presented with its opportunity for power in 1958, it was ready for the task.
Exile had sharpened its organization and its leadership,
and in spite of myriad problems at home and a determined
effort by the Castro regime to unseat them, the Adecos
were able to govern and reform Venezuelan society
through the difficult years of 1958-1963. Romulo
Betancourt was, in some ways a visionary reformer, in
that he knew what he wanted for his fatherland. At the

same time, however, he went about the business of organizing a political party as if his political life depended on it (and it did). Ramón Grau San Martín was also a visionary politician, and his vision for his _patria_ was much the same as was Betancourt's. The difference, and the tragedy for Cuba, was that Grau, unlike Betancourt, thought that vision could be translated into reality with words, and not with organization.

Notes

1. Hugh Thomas, Cuba: The Pursuit of Freedom. (New York: Harper and Row, 1971), 605.

2. Luis Aguilar, Cuba 1933: Prologue to Revolution. (Ithaca: Cornell University Press), 231.

3. The Amendment, originally tacked on to the Military Appropriations Bill of 1902 by Senator Orville Platt of the Foreign Relations Committee, was later incorporated into the Cuban Constitution of 1903. It gave the United States the right to intervene unilaterally in Cuban affairs "for the preservation of Cuban independence and the maintenance of stable government...."

4. Aguilar, 61.

5. Ibid., 157.

6. President Roosevelt felt, with some justification, that if Caffery were sent as Ambassador, this would imply recognition of the Grau government by the United States.

7. United States, Government Printing Office, United States Foreign Relations: II, 1933. (Washington: USGPO, 1958), 417.

8. Ruby Hart Phillips, Cuban Sideshow. (Havana, n.p., 1933), 73.

9. Jose A. Tabares del Real, La Revolucion del 30: Sus Dos Ultimos Años. (La Habana: Editorial de Ciencias Sociales, 1973), 151.

10. Thomas, 737.

11. The details of Grau's life are taken from the following sources: Thomas; Aguilar; Carleton Beals, The Crime of Cuba. (Philadelphia: J. B. Lippincott Company, 1933); Ramon Eduardo Ruiz, Cuba: The Making of a Revolution. (New York: W.W. Norton Company, 1970); Russel H. Fitzgibbon, Cuba and the United States: 1900-1935. (New York: Russell and Russell, 1964); and especially, Irwin F. Gellman, Roosevelt and Batista. (Albuquerque: University of New Mexico Press, 1973).

12. Aguilar, 170.

13. Gellman, 56.

14. Jorge I. Dominquez, Cuba: Order and Revolution. (Cambridge, Mass.: Harvard University Press, 1978), 109.

15. Aguilar, 170-171.

16. Thomas, 650.

17. Ruiz, 85.

8
Indo-Americanism in Peru

The political ideas of Victor Raul Haya de la Torre
have resounded throughout Latin America since the early
part of the twentieth century.[1] His writings have had
a profound influence, not only in his native Peru, but
in every country of the continent with a substantial
Indian population. His political philosophy, based on a
concept of a united America with a culture based upon a
melding of Indian and European elements, has had great
appeal to untold numbers of political practitioners and
masses of people through the years.[2] Yet, Haya de la
Torre and his mass-based political party, the Alianza
Popular Revolucionaria Americana (APRA--Popular Revolutionary American Alliance, hereafter referred to by its
popular name, APRA) have never been successful in
capturing the government of Peru, the nation in which
the movement began and the base of Haya's political
career for over sixty years. APRA is undoubtedly the
largest, most popular, and best-organized political
party in Latin America never to come to power within the
political processes of its own nation. Various
explanations have been offered for this failure of APRA
to achieve what is the goal of every organized political
party in the world. Was the relative failure of APRA to
achieve political success due, as Harry Kantor has
suggested, to the fact that "...they have been faced by
a long-established, implacable, ruthless foe which looks
back to four hundred years of class domination and cannot comprehend an order in which it does not rule."[3]
Certainly, as the following quick overview of recent
Peruvian history will show, there is a great deal of
truth in Kantor's statement. Or, was APRA's failure due
to the essential passivity of the Peruvian Indians who,
while not constituting the vanguard of the Aprista movement, were at least supposed to be the foot soldiers of
the new order? The Indians, however, never responded in
the numbers imagined by Haya and his colleagues.
Instead, "Illiterate, superstitious, debilitated,
poverty-stricken, and exploited for generations..." the

Indians in the Peruvian highlands remained largely aloof
from the political movement whose ideology was predicated on their political ascendancy.[4]

A third possible explanation for APRA's failure,
offered by the Peruvian right, was its international
character. APRA was regarded as a "social cancer" by
many in the Peruvian oligarchy, at least in part because
its program called for a breaking down of national
boundaries and the development of a continental culture
based in large part on the existing Indian culture in
the western hemisphere.[5] Finally, it has been
suggested that part of APRA's failure was due to the
limitations of its leader, Haya de la Torre. Rarely has
any political movement been so totally dominated for
such a long period of time by one man as was APRA from
the 1920s until the late 1970s. During that time, as we
shall see, Haya forged a near-monopoly of personal power
within the councils of APRA, so that the Party came to
represent the lengthened shadow of one man, rather than
becoming the rather impersonal political machine one
might expect to develop over such a long period of
time:

> By some standards, Haya's career has been an
> unsuccessful one. Although his party has been
> a major contender for power for over four
> decades, and although he himself has been an
> aspirant for the presidency of Peru for almost
> as long, neither he nor his party has ever come
> to power.

> The reasons for the Apristas' failure to
> achieve what is presumably the objective of
> every political party, power, are numerous, and
> this is not the place to explore many of them.
> However, at least part of the failure of the
> Apristas is due to Haya's own weaknesses as a
> practical politician.[6]

In the following pages we hope to examine what is
one of the most significant failures of institution-
building in Latin America in the twentieth century.

The Environment

Interestingly (and significantly) the Alianza
Popular Revolucionaria Americana was not founded in
Peru. Instead, on May 7, 1924, Victor Raul Haya de la
Torre and several other student leaders in exile in
Mexico City established the party that was destined to
play a major role in Peruvian politics for decades to
come. Haya had been exiled from Peru a year earlier
when, as a student leader at the University of San

Marcos in Lima, he and others had protested the attempt by President-dictator Augusto B. Leguia to dedicate the nation of Peru to the Sacred Heart of Jesus.

Haya and Leguia were players during a time of considerable turbulence in Peruvian and Latin American affairs. World War I had affected Peruvian society as it had almost every other Latin American nation. Suddenly, because of the War, the nation's easy dependence upon manufactured goods from Europe and North America was interrupted. The result was the development of a beginning industrial plant in the coastal areas of northern and central Peru. Trujillo in the north and the Lima - Callao urban mass in central Peru began to develop rapidly as urban centers in what had been, up to then, largely an agricultural nation. In addition, the War increased world demand for Peru's largely agricultural and mining products. The opening of the Panama Canal in 1914 made the delivery of these materials to European and North American markets much easier and less expensive than had heretofore been the case.

Specific elements within Peruvian society began to organize and make their influence felt during the years following the World War. Labor, largely under the influence of the anarcho-syndicalist movement emanating from Europe, began to organize in the face of determined opposition from the entrenched elite. The European origin of the Peruvian labor movement meant that their goals were more political than were the goals of the American Federation of Labor in the United States. Strikes, while not always successful, became more commonplace in Peru following World War I. Students, heretofore a largely unorganized group, began organizing for political action even before World War I, and by 1916 had formed the Peruvian Student Federation, the first national student organization with avowedly political goals.

Peru's Indian population, which formed between one-third and one-half of the entire population of the country, was concentrated primarily in the Andean third of the nation. The Indians of Peru had never been as quiescent as suggested by some historians, and serious revolts had occurred in the Andean region in the late nineteenth century. Most of these had, however, been of a transitory nature, and it was not until the demand for Peruvian wool increased rapidly after the turn of the century that the Indians began to react to their continued oppression in an organized way. This growing turmoil among the Indians concatenated with the rise of the Indigenista movement among the educated elite in the coastal zone. Although the movement never achieved the full political and social expression that it did in Mexico it nevertheless was to play an important role in the thinking of various influential individuals for the rest of the twentieth century in Peru.

All of the above is not to suggest that Peru suddenly became a modern nation in the early decades of the twentieth century. Nothing could be further from the truth. The nascent labor movement, the growing student organizations, and the rise of social and political consciousness among the Indians and their supporters were all limited to small numbers of people in a population still dominated by a centuries-old Hispanic culture, ruled vigorously by a small, white, wealthy elite, with the assistance of the Peruvian military. Peru after World War I had begun to experience the process of modernization, but the process was to remain agonizingly slow for decades to come. While Mexico, Argentina, and other Latin American nations were experiencing full-blown crises of participation, legitimacy, and integration, Peru was entering the preliminary stages of these crises. By almost any objective index Peru was far behind most other large Latin American nations in social mobilization. It would be difficult if not impossible to make a case that the "objective" conditions for political party development existed in Peru in the years after World War I.

Yet, ideas have a force of their own. And in the relatively arid soil of Peruvian society, certain ideas espoused by individual thinkers sprang up and exerted an influence on subsequent Peruvian history. Certainly, the father of Peruvian radicalism and the intellectual forebear of subsequent Peruvian political thinkers (including both Carlos Mariategui and Victor Raul Haya de la Torre, the two great Peruvian radicals of the twentieth century) was Manuel Gonzalez Prada (1848-1918). Gonzalez Prada's philosophy is impossible to categorize. He was not a Marxist, yet he rejected western capitalism in all its forms. He believed that Peru's vindication would come from its Indian masses, yet he rejected Indianismo as paternalistic. "The Indian will be saved," he said, "thanks to his own efforts."[7] Although Gonzales Prada's philosophy was difficult, he nevertheless exerted a great influence on the new, often middle-class students in the rapidly expanding university system. His broadside attacks on the Church ("idolatry"), the army ("a mountain where a man climbs by kissing the ass of the man ahead of him, while being kissed in the same place by the man who follows"), and the nation itself (Peru was "an immense boil. Press down anywhere and pus runs out") were legendary. Prada's influence on generations of university students, who perceived the truth of much of what he was saying, was immense, even though conditions were not "ripe" for the development of institutions to carry out the reforms indicated by such a view.[8]

As elsewhere in Latin America, the established elite reacted to this perceived threat to their continued rule of Peruvian society. The indigenista movement was countered by an equally strong hispanista group, who often deprecated the Indians as little more than beasts of burden, holding back the development of a modern Peru along the lines of classical Hispanic society.

The accelerated pace of economic development and the attendant social change after 1914 placed a severe strain on the Peruvian political system. New entrepreneurs who had amassed their wealth through modern capitalism challenged the power of the old elites. Meanwhile, strategically placed groups--students, industrial workers and middle-class managers, technicians, civil servants, and white-collar employees--expanded in numbers and became increasingly politicized. From the right and the left of the political spectrum and from the top to the bottom of the socio-economic pyramid, Peruvians demanded greater government concern for their needs and aspirations.[9]

A broad view of Peruvian history for most of the twentieth century could perceive that history as a continuing struggle, almost a civil war, between two major groups; those who wished to maintain the status quo and those who wished to modernize the nation to include within the effective nation those groups who thus far had not had access to it. This same broad view of history would conclude that, up to now, those fighting for the status quo have won. Peru has not yet had either a substantive reform of its society or its alternative, a social revolution. Certainly, a major reason for this outcome has been the reaction, beginning concurrently with the increased demands described above, of a well-entrenched elite, convinced of its right to continue rule, and backed by the military, economic, social and political power at its command.

As elsewhere in Latin America the Peruvian elite responded almost immediately to this threat to their continued rule of society. Labor organizations and their activities were met with extreme hostility and repression, and many strikes were put down by government troops. The students were tolerated to a greater degree than were the workers, probably for two reasons. First, many students were the sons and daughters of the elite, and their university radicalism was widely regarded (often correctly) as simply a passing phase of youthful exuberance. Second, the students in most instances failed to connect with the workers and Indians whose cause they espoused. Thus, their radical verbiage remained suspended in the air of the classrooms at San Marcos and other universities throughout the country. When, as was the case in 1919, students and workers were able to make common cause in a protest movement, the elite responded forcefully against both groups.

The first and perhaps the most signal action taken by the elite against the new groups was the ouster, on Feburary 4, 1914, of President Guillermo Billinghurst. Billinghurst had been elected in 1912 on a platform of reforms designed to benefit the common people as well as the elite. Once in office, Billinghurst embarked upon a number of projects designed to implement at least some of his campaign rhetoric. More ominously, from the view of the elite, Billinghurst made common cause with the nation's nascent labor movement and also with the largely unorganized urban prolatariat. Time after time, in the years between 1912 and 1914, mobs of workers would storm an unfriendly newspaper, or would demonstrate outside a Congress still controlled by representatives of the old elitist parties. The rules of the Peruvian political game up to then had permitted the President to use the army in his differences with the Congress, but the use of mobs by Billinghurst introduced a new, and terrifying, element into Peruvian politics. These were the dispossessed hungering for power, and they finally had a President who was willing to use them for his own ends. The old political compact was in danger of being ruptured. Finally, in 1914, the Congress refused to authorize the budget for that year. Billinghurst responded by authorizing government expenditures by presidential decree, meanwhile calling for the replacement of Congress by an assembly representative of the will of the people. Finally, the army, which had hitherto been unwilling to proceed in a coup against their commander in chief, learned that Billingshurst planned to arm the workers and dissolve the Congress by decree. The President had gone too far, and on the morning of February 4, 1914, Billinghurst was ousted from the presidential palace.

The coup differed in kind from previous military interventions in Peruvian politics. First, it ended almost two decades of reduced military interference in government, and brought the military back to the center of Peruvian politics, where it has remained ever since. Second, the coup was not, as coups had been in the past, simply a matter of the military taking sides for or against one personality within the ruling elite. This time, the military intervened as an institution.

> ...to rescue the elite-dominated political system from a threat by the urban working class. During the next several decades the Peruvian armed forces continued to identify their own institutional interests with those of the changing upper class.[10]

The coup eventually brought to power, as the repre-

sentative of the elite, the man who had preceded
Billinghurst in office--Augusto Bernardo Leguía y
Salcedo. Leguía proceeded to rule Peru in an increasingly autocratic manner for the next eleven years until
his eventual overthrow by the armed forces in 1930.
The oncenio, and Leguía himself, have been widely discussed and analysed. Suffice to say that the historical
consensus is that modern Peru came into being during the
oncenio and that Leguia, for all his faults, laid the
groundwork for a modern Peru. The dictator poured
government money into various modernization projects,
including roads, sewers, and irrigation. Little of the
investment filtered down to the lower socio-economic
groups, but the Peruvian economy began to boom during
the period. Production of sugar, cotton, and other
agricultural products doubled. Mining production sky-
rocketed, with petroleum and copper leading the way.
Leguia, an admirer of the United States, encouraged
foreign investment in much of the country's basic
industries, setting the stage for later disputes over
the extent and nature of this investment. The 1920s in
Peru were a time of laissez-faire capitalism, and for
the time at least, it appeared that this type of national development would succeed in Peru. The dark spots
were there, however, and eventually led to the collapse
of much of Peru's economic progress during the decade
and to the downfall of Leguia himself. The world prices
for Peru's major exports simply did not rise as fast as
the exports themselves, so Peru seemed to be on a
treadmill, exporting more and more but receiving less in
foreign exchange for these increased exports. Further,
although Leguía himself did not apparently profit from
his oncenio, those around him (including his two sons)
did. At the same time, the profits being reaped were
not shared by the majority of the population, so Leguia
had no constituency among the proletariat, once the
elite decided to remove him. And finally, the 1929
crash and the world depression put a definitive end to
Peru's dreams of a golden age. Peru was in deep debt to
the New York banks, her export prices had plummeted
sharply, and to compound matters, Leguía was being
accused of selling out the fatherland in diplomatic
settlements with Chile and Colombia.

The 1930 army coup, however, was designed to assure
the continuation of elitist rule in Peru rather than to
oust an entire ruling class. The political history of
Peru in the 1930s was dismal. The elections of 1931,
still disputed to this day, brought to power the leader
of the coup that ousted Leguía, Army Colonel Manuel
Sanchez Cerro. Sanchez was assassinated by an Aprista
activist in 1933, and Congress elected as his successor
Oscar A. Benavides, who proceeded to rule the country
from 1933 to 1939. For these six years, relations
between APRA, which had now become a major force in

Peruvian politics, and the government swung wildly from cooperation (convivencia, as it was known in Peru) to outright hostility and repression. This pattern was to continue throughout the next five decades, with the armed forces in the background implacably opposed to APRA's gaining power. All presidents had to tread the line between APRA and the military, and usually came down on the side of the military. APRA's tactics during the period, which swung from participation in elections, through abstention, to planning for revolution, have often been cited as a major reason for the determined opposition by the armed forces and the elite. On the other hand, the tactics of the elite, in denying APRA the chance to come to power legitimately, contributed to the sense of desperation and frustration which the Aprista leaders experienced. Each side fed the worst fears of the other, with the result that each side became ever more determined to use any and all means against its opponents. The result, of course, was inevitable. The army had most of the guns, while APRA was essentially unarmed. APRA could never generate enough appeal among the Indian masses to offset the army's and the elite's advantages in organization and force. The result was over fifty years of frustration for what was probably, during most of this period, the largest and best-organized political party in Peru.

The Leader

The literature on Victor Raul Haya de la Torre and APRA is immense.[11] Both the man and the party have captured the imagination of Latin Americans and North Americans alike. The reasons for this phenomenon are not hard to discern. First, the man was an extremely interesting subject for biographers. Any person who plays a pivotal role in the politics of his country for more than fifty years is deserving of extensive biographical treatment. Second, Haya's pretensions (never realized) toward a hemispheric political and social movement made him even more intriguing to biographers. Third, Haya as a person aroused strong passions both inside Peru and in other countries of the hemisphere. Thus we have a number of biographical treatments that fall into the categories of hagiography or character assassination. Finally, Haya's political and social philosophy, quoting freely as he does from Toynbee and others, is deserving of extensive treatment, and has been accorded that treament in a number of tomes. What follows here is, of course, merely a partial biography. We are interested in the philosophy of Haya and APRA only in so far as it bears upon the success of the leader and his party in attaining political success. Those who are interested in a detailed examination of the admittedly fascinating philosophy developed by Haya should look elsewhere.

Victor Raul Haya de la Torre was born, on February 22, 1895, in Trujillo, a major city in the north of Peru. His father was Raul Edmundo Haya y Cárdenas, and his mother was Zoila Victoria de la Torre y Cárdenas. They had been married on April 24 the previous year, by Zoila's uncle who was Dean of the Cathedral of Trujillo. Victor Raul's father was a newspaperman, intensely interested in public affairs, and young Victor Raul grew up in a home full of political talk. Although Haya's biographers like to expound on the noble lineage in his family, the truth is that, by the time Victor Raul was born, his father had, along with many other residents of the Norte, fallen on comparatively hard times. Raul Edmundo, who had previously been the publisher of the local newspaper was now forced to work as a reporter for the same enterprise. Later, the elder Haya sought work on one of the large sugar plantations in the area, owned by U.S. and German interests. Nevertheless, Victor Raul grew up in what could be described as middle-class sur-roundings, even though at times this existence was precarious. In spite of the reduced circumstances of the immediate family, several of Victor Raul's cousins had been able to retain much of their wealth. Quite probably, as is the case in many Latin American societies, these cousins contributed to the support of their less fortunate relatives. On a number of occa-sions, Victor Raul was dressed up and sent to visit with his wealthier relatives. His biographers record that he was not impressed, but to the contrary, began to wonder why these less-than-distinguished individuals had all their money.[12]

Victor Raul's early schooling took place in Trujillo, where he was sent to the best school in the city, the Seminary of San Carlos, run by the Lazarist Fathers. Victor Raul was a good student, but his interests lay outside the classroom. Music and arche-ology, along with an interest in politics at an early age, consumed most of his outside hours. In September, 1908, while on a school picnic, Victor Raul asked permission to return to the city to get the news of the latest transfer of power in the presidency. One of his teachers, a Frenchman, asked why Victor Raul was in such haste. "Because the news from Lima about the transfer of power should have arrived," answered the thirteen year old. "And what do you have to do with politics, little one?" "Oh," answered Victor Raul, "politics interests me very much!"[13]

In 1913, having graduated from the Seminary with his bachillerato, Victor Raul enrolled in the National University of Trujillo. He almost immediately became a member of a small group of middle-class young men who founded a literary club. "The literary rebellion was an

126

escape valve..." for young men of the middle-class; for
the Universities were still the refuge of the elite,
with few middle-class students enrolled.[14] Haya remained at the university in Trujillo for four years, but
then an unexpected small inheritance allowed him to
transfer to the University of San Marcos, in Lima, where
he finally enrolled in 1918. San Marcos was (and still
is) the center of higher education in Peru. The oldest
university in the western hemisphere, it had a reputation second to none in the country. San Marcos was
also, however, still populated mainly by the sons and
daughters of the elite, so that Victor Raul found
himself once again a member of a small group of middle-
class radicals, but this time radicals whose influence
was widening rapidly within university circles. It was
at San Marcos, too, that Victor Raul met Manuel Gonzalez
Prada, the grand old radical of Peruvian political
thought. It was also at San Marcos that Haya met and
befriended a thin, asthmatic young man named Carlos
Mariátegui, who was to become Peru's greatest Marxist
philosopher. In such an atmosphere, Haya's political
career blossomed. He quickly established himself within
the inner circle of the Peruvian Student Federation, and
in 1919 was elected president of the organization. He
spent the next three years working at night as a teacher
in the Colegio Anglo-Peruano school operated by a Pres-
byterian minister. During the day, Haya was busy forg-
ing coalitions that would permit him to enter national
politics. He began to travel widely, representing the
Student Federation at conferences in Montevideo, Buenos
Aires, and Santiago.

Finally, in 1923, Haya's opportunity to make a name
for himself presented itself. In that year, the dictator Augusto Leguía decided to dedicate the Republic of
Peru to the Sacred Heart of Jesus. Although Haya had,
along with most of his compatriots, supported Leguia
back in 1919, he now broke definitively with the dictator. He was the principal organizer of a mass rally
protesting Leguía's action and, when troops broke up the
rally and killed a student, Haya was the principal
speaker the next day at the student's funeral. Troops
also dispersed this gathering. Haya escaped from the
dragnet, but was finally captured and imprisoned in
October. After a week of student protests, Leguia
decided to deport Victor Raul, who then left Peru, not
to return for eight years.

Haya's eight year odyssey was of the mind as well
as the body. "When he left Peru in 1923, his ideological baggage consisted of elementary Marxism and a few
amorphous ideas about social justice, nationalism, and
revolution."[15] During his stays in Mexico, the
Soviet Union, Switzerland, Italy, France, and finally
Great Britain, Haya developed and then refined the
essential doctrine of _Aprismo_, rejecting both western

capitalism and Marxism, and searching for a third way to achieve the liberation of the masses of Latin America. He also spent a great deal of time attempting to organize and publicize his new political party, which had been proclaimed publicly during his first visit to Mexico in 1924. In January, 1928, Haya announced the formation of the Peruvian Nationalist Party, an affiliate of APRA, and announced that he would run against Leguia in the elections scheduled for 1929. The announcement and campaign were in reality no more than a subterfuge, as Aprista activists in the Norte prepared for a revolution against Leguia. However, the revolutionary plans went awry, and Haya, instead of returning to Peru, was forced to spend the rest of his exile in Germany. Haya finally returned to Peru in 1931, after the departure from office of both Leguia and Sanchez Cerro (who thought all Apristas were communists, and therefore should be killed). He immediately declared for the presidency in the elections to be held later that year. Haya's main opponent was the former dictator, Sanchez Cerro. After a spirited campaign, in which charges of fraud were hurled by the Apristas, Sanchez Cerro was declared the winner. Although later, more moderate scholarship has shown the election to be basically honest, at the time the Apristas believed they had been cheated. A series of violent events now followed, culminating in another failed revolution by the Apristas. Due in large part to a growing conviction that Haya and APRA would stop at nothing to gain political power, Sanchez Cerro and his allies among the elite pushed through the Constitution of 1933, with its Article 53 banning political parties of "international organization." This, of course, restricted APRA's participation in Peruvian politics for several decades. As if in retaliation, a young Aprista shot and killed Sanchez Cerro as he was reviewing the troops in Lima, on April 30, 1933.

The new Peruvian government, under the leadership of former provisional president and army General Oscar Benavides, now attempted to deal with the Aprista problem through a policy of moderation. Talks were held, proposals and counter-proposals were made, all to naught. By now, the Party had organized in a much more militaristic fashion. All power was granted to Haya and his associates in the Central Executive Committee (CEN). In later years, other individuals would hold the post of Secretary-General, while Victor Raul became the "Supreme Chief" above party organization, much in the manner of Mao Zedong in his later years in China. Another failed Aprista revolt in 1934 led to nearly a decade of hiding for the party's Supreme Chief, but he continued his manifestos and organizing activities while eluding the Peruvian military and police.

Benavides left the presidency in 1939, after

elections (in which APRA could not participate) brought Manual Prado to the presidency. For the next six years, events seemed to be moving toward some form of compromise within Peruvian politics. APRA began to modify its radical rhetoric, and Haya himself seemed to be more friendly toward western style democracy than he had been. Perhaps the spectacle of the imperalist yanquis fighting against Fascism inspired Haya. At the same time, Benavides now tried to bring some domestic peace to Peru, and finally achieved his purpose with an agreement with Haya that neither would participate in the presidential elections of 1945. In mid-May, APRA, now under the name Partido de Pueblo because of the strictures of the 1933 Constitution, was granted legal status. Later that year, in free elections, Jose Luis Bustamante y Rivero won the presidency with the backing of both Haya and Benavides. APRA, meanwhile, won a resounding victory in the congressional elections, and looked ahead confidently to the presidential elections of 1951 when, they were certain, victory would be theirs at last.

This was not to be, however, during the ensuing three years, the party that Haya had so carefully built began to fall apart. Ideological differences between the old guard, now officially friendly to the United States, and the new left within the Party, began to appear. Haya, at age fifty, began to show signs of early senility, at least to his critics. Finally, paramilitary units within APRA, encouraged initially by Haya, began to plan yet another coup against the government. After a series of events in which Haya and his advisers, in consultation with military units who were planning their own coup, agreed to postpone the Aprista effort, young Aprista militants went ahead with their own abortive revolutionary attempt. The would-be revolutionaries were pounded into submission while Haya and his advisers stood on the sidelines, and President Bustamante once again outlawed APRA:

> Troops seized the party's headquarters, newspapers, and radio stations. Within a week more than 1,000 Aprista leaders had been arrested. APRA's top officials charged the authors of the revolt with treacherous insubordination. The perpetrators of the uprising and other militants accused Haya and his advisers of cowardice and treason. The party was in shambles.[16]

After all this, the military did strike against the civilian government, and by the end of 1948 APRA, which had contributed mightily to its own problems, was on the ropes once again. By the late 1950s, however, after the dismantling of the Odria dictatorship, APRA once again made a comeback of sorts by cooperating with a presidential aspirant of another political group. This time it was Manuel Prado, who won a close election in 1956 with APRA support, and who responded by once again legalizing the Party. This time, however, APRA was not aligning itself with the most progressive political force in the election. A new face had appeared on the Peruvian political scene: Fernando Belaunde y Terry, Dean of the San Marcos School of Architecture and scion of a wealthy Arequipa family. Belaunde had entered politics on a platform similar to APRA's, and was regarded by Haya and the Apristas as a usurper of their ideology. In a sense, the charge was true, but by 1956 APRA had made so many detours in its political journey that it was sometimes difficult to ascertain what its ideology was. Although Belaunde lost the 1956 election, he gained lustre through his own efforts, and also through the political deal between APRA and the oligarchy. APRA did gain a modicum of political power during the next six years, but by the time of the 1962 presidential election. APRA was becoming more and more tainted by its rightist association:

> APRA did acquire greater acceptability among the nations's upper class. Prior to the 1962 election one prominent rightist described Haya de la Torre as 'the conservative leader this country needs.' But the party paid dearly for this new respectability, losing much of its already diminished radical wing. The rise of Fidel Castro...hastened the disintegration of the APRA left. At its fourth national congress in 1959, the party purged eight leaders who expressed opposition to the convivencia with Prado. The next year, APRA lost control of the Peruvian Student Federation to a new leftist coalition....During the campaign Haya found himself in the awkward position of being welcomed in conservative circles while his appeals to former supporters on the left were met with skepticism and even open hostility.[17]

Even so, it appears tha Haya and APRA did at last achieve an electoral victory in the 1962 elections. Final returns, as reported in the Lima press, gave Haya 32.98 percent of the vote to Belaunde's 32.1 percent. Former dictator Odria gained 28.45 percent, while minor party candidates accounted for the rest. However, since Haya had not received the one-third of the votes required for direct election, the contest would now be decided by a majority of the combined membership of the new parliament, which was itself seriously divided. At this juncture, the military intervened once again. Deposing President Prado, the army declared the election

results null and void, and for the next year proceeded
to govern the country, while preparing for new
elections, which were finally held in late 1963. Once
again, the election was a three-man contest among
Belaunde, Haya de la Torre, and Odria. This time,
Belaunde won a clear victory, and what proved to be
Haya's last chance of the presidency went glimmering.
Haya reacted to his loss by refusing to join forces with
Belaunde in the new congress, but rather made a pact
with Odria to block Belaunde's program in the legislature. This latest action appalled even many die-hard
Apristas, as Odria represented what were probably the
worst elements of reaction in Peruvian society.
Belaunde, unable to govern effectively, hung on to power
almost to the end of his term, but was deposed by an
army coup in 1968. For the next twelve years, the army
as an institution ruled Peru, in what came to be described as a "Nasserist" dictatorship. The doctrine of
"Participianismo" espoused by these unlikely reformers
in uniform intrigues many people, both in and out of
Peru, but the result, as far as APRA was concerned, was
to exclude them from any further participation in
politics during the period of army rule. In addition,
the military, which had moved to the left as APRA had
moved to the right, proceeded to implement many of the
reforms of Peruvian society earlier advocated by a
younger and more vital Haya de la Torre. By the time
the dictatorship ended in 1980, and new presidential
elections were held, Victor Raul Haya de la Torre had
died at the age of 84, without ever realizing his dream
of gaining the presidency of Peru, and APRA appeared to
have lost much of its driving force, as former president
Fernando Belaunde Terry, who had organized a potent
political organization (Acción Popular--Popular Action,
AP) around his considerable charisma, swept back into
the presidency in that year.

What went wrong? In retrospect, three things stand
out. First, APRA in Peru encountered an entrenched
elite--powerful, sure of itself, and willing to use any
means to perpetuate its power over a long period of
time. Perhaps the political party in Latin America
which comes closest to APRA, at least in its historical
development, is Acción Democrática in Venezuela. Yet,
AD succeeded in gaining political power where APRA did
not. In its formative years, AD was forced to fight
against an entrenched elite, much as APRA was. The
difference lay, however, in the nature of those elites.
The Venezuelan elite was simply not as entrenched in its
power, not as sure of itself, not as willing to use any
means to perpetuate its rule as was the Peruvian elite.
History, geographical location, and ethnicity all come
into play here. While Peru was, in colonial times, the
center of the Spanish empire in the New World, Venezuela
was but an outpost. Thus, the tradition of Hispanidad,

the reverence for Spanish culture and civilization, with its concomitant scorn for Indian or mestizo values, never gained as much acceptance in Venezuela as it did in Peru. Lima is, today, one of the most "Spanish" cities in Latin America, while Caracas is simply a booming modernizing, junior-grade metropolis in the Third World, with no discernible Spanish stamp.

Venezuela, because of its location closer to Europe and North America, was an easier target for intellectual currents emanating from these two metropoli. Francisco Miranda, the intellectual precursor of the great revolutions against Spain at the beginning of the nineteenth century, and Simon Bolivar were both from Caracas, and this was not historical accident. Rather, these men and others tasted the heady wine of both the French and American revolutions, and the ideas they engendered, long before those ideas finally swept down the west coast of South America. After the Revolution, the idea of a fixed ruling class, based on Hispanidad, never took hold in Venezuela as it did in Peru. The idea of a natural elite, born to govern, was always sharply contradicted by intellectual currents from the north and east.

Finally Peru, unlike Venezuela, is a nation with a large Indian population, culturally defined. This group has alternately been despised and feared by the small elite--Spanish and a few mestizos--who have ruled the nation. Venezuela, on the other hand, is predominantly mestizo. The racial-ethnic differences between Perez Jimenez and Rómulo Betancourt were not apparent (if they indeed existed) and played no role in their political and ideological differences. Peru, however, confirms that race is still a powerful force in politics in the Western Hemisphere.

It is a major thesis of this book that the environment affects but does not control the specific political outcome of political development or decay. Such was the case in Peru. Given the hostile environment, Haya de la Torre and his lieutenants made several egregious political errors which were largely avoided by their counterparts in Venezuela. First, APRA had little constancy of purpose or tactic. Its first move as a political party was to attempt a revolution in 1928; and thereafter it alternated between attempts to win through the ballot box and new revolutionary attempts. In so doing, it poisoned the well of Peruvian politics. The elite became convinced--truly convinced--that APRA was not merely another political party, but rather a revolutionary movement bent on the overturn of the existing social order. At the same time, APRA misread the enthusiasms of the middle-class for revolutionary overturn and the elite was able to use APRA's misdirected revolutionary attempts in convincing substantial portions of the middle-class that APRA was not to be trusted. In short, APRA's commitment to the democratic process was not as constant nor as massive as was AD's, and this hurt its chances for success by confirming the worst fears of the elite and affording propaganda opportunities for its enemies.

Much of the difference in approach has to be laid at the doorstep of Victor Raul Haya de la Torre. He simply did not possess the patient, organizational political personality of Romula Betancourt. Where Betancourt in hiding and in exile was constantly organizing and waiting for his opportunity at the ballot box, Haya appeared to be increasingly consumed by his ideology, and less and less concerned with the creation of a political party acceptable or at least tolerable to all elements of Peruvian society. Perhaps, as suggested by Harry Kantor, this was an impossible task in Peru, but the point is that Haya never made the same deter- mined, long-range effort that Betancourt made in Venezuela to create what Betancourt called a Multi- clasista political party.

APRA's lack of constancy, as compared to that of AD, also manifested itself in its willingness to join with groups of all political persuasions for what amounted to temporary political advantage. Haya's pact with former dictator Odria was certainly the most in- famous of these political deals, but it was not the only questionable alliance entered into by APRA. By con- trast, AD steadfastly refused to cooperate with what it regarded as the forces of reaction within the country, even though opportunities did present themselves. The contrast is obvious. APRA sullied its democratic re- formist image and alienated many of its more idealistic followers by entering into what were regarded by many as pacts with the devil. Morality aside, this simply was poor politics, and once again was probably tied up with Haya's consuming desire to become president of Peru at any cost. Once again, an individual ego got in the way of good political strategy.

Finally, the continued insistence of Haya that he and only he be the presidential candidate of the Party in election after election probably cost the Party the presidency in 1963, at least. In the earlier 1962 elections, subsequently annulled by the army, Haya's lieutenant Manuel Seoane had outpolled Haya as the Party's Vice-Presidential candidate; and many in the Party thought that Seoane, not Haya, should be the Party's candidate for President in 1963. In addition, Seoane was more acceptable to the armed forces, and therefore many voters, who felt they were throwing away their vote for Haya (the army would never let him take office even if he were elected) would have voted for Seoane. The Seoane candidacy was not to be, however, as Haya was once again duly nominated by the Party faithful.

The genesis of these political miscalculations lay in the realm of Haya de la Torre's political personalality. He had become accustomed, in his early life, to getting what he wanted (<u>mimado</u>, in Spanish), and this attitude carried over into his political career. Haya's family evidently made extraordinary sacrifices to see to it that he received the best education then available, and he rose rapidly to the top in student politics. Betancourt, on the other hand, was distinctly a follower in his student days. He was never president of the student federation, and at the big student rallies he was one of a number of speakers, rather than the one who harangued the crowd.

There were similarities in the lives of the two leaders. Both were from middle-class provincial families, but Betancourt's parents had not fallen upon recent hard times as had Haya's. Both went to the University, but Haya made a career of it, whereas Betancourt, while involved in politics at the University level, graduated within the prescribed period of time. Both men wrote about politics, but Haya's writings consume seven volumes, and constitute a full-blown ideology, while Betancourt's writings were relatively brief and his ideology relatively inchoate. The great difference in the two lives, and the one that overshadows all other similarities and differences, is that, because of their different political personalities, Betancourt succeeded and Haya failed in their quests for political power. In so doing, Betancourt bequeathed Venezuela not only an institutionalized political party, but one of the more stable democracies in today's Latin America. That Peru today enjoys a tenuous democracy is due more to Fernando Belaunde than to Victor Raul Haya de la Torre.

134

Notes

1. See Harry Kantor, The Ideology and Program of the Peruvian APRISTA Movement (New York: Octagon Books, 1966), for a good summary of Haya's political ideas and their influence in Latin America.
2. Robert J. Alexander (ed.) APRISMO: The Ideas and Doctrines of Victor Raul Haya de la Torre (Kent, OH: Kent State University Press, 1973), 52-63.
3. Kantor, 21.
4. R. J. Owens, Peru (London: Oxford University Press, 1963), 93.
5. Manuel Cesar de la Guardia, Aprismo: Cancer Social (Santiago, Chile: Editorial Indoamericana, 1938), is a good example of this frantic opposition to APRA and its leader.
6. Alexander, 20.
7. David W. Werlich, Peru: A Short History (Carbondale, IL: Southern Illinois University Press, 1978), 144.
8. Prada was probably closer to a philosophical anarchist than he was to any other coherent political philosophy.
9. Werlich, 147.
10. Ibid.
11. In addition to the books by Kantor and Alexander listed above, sources of Haya's life include: Percy Murillo Garaycochea, Historia de APRA: 1919-1945 (Lima: Imprenta Editora Atlantida, S.A., 1977); Luis Alberto Sanchez, Haya de la Torre o el Politico: Cronica de Una Vida Sin Tregua (Santiago, Chile: Ediciones Erilla, 1934); F. Cossio del Pomar, Haya de la Torre el Indoamericano (Mexico: Editorial America, 1939); Tibaldo Gonzalez, Haya de la Torre: Trayectoria de Una Ideologia (Caracas: Tipografia Garrido, 1958); Felipe Cossio del Pomar, Victor Raul: Biografia de Haya de la Torre (Mexico: Editorial Cultura, 1961); C.A. Guardia Mayorga, Construyendo el Aprismo (Arequipa, Peru: Tipografia Acosta, 1945); Luis Alberto Sanchez, Biografia del APRA (Lima: Mosca Azul Editores, 1978); and Victor Raul Haya de la Torre, Obras Completas: Vol's 1-7 (Lima: Libreria - Editorial Juan Mejia Baca, 1976).
12. Cossio, 24-30.
13. Ibid.
14. Gonzalez, 29.
15. Werlich, 182.
16. Ibid., 245.
17. Ibid., 267-268.

9
The Autumn of the Patriarch

President Reagan states that the current warfare in El Salvador is due to a concerted communist threat aimed at taking over Central America. Congressmen and others counter with the assertion that the warfare in El Salvador grows out of a long history of abuses of the civilian population by a brutal military, plus underlying social inequalities. Historians and political scientists try to discern what the true forces are at work in El Salvador today. In the process, the name of the man who contributed mightily to the current events in that unhappy country is lost. General Maximiliano Hernandez Martinez (always referred to as General Martinez) ruled the nation of El Salvador for thirteen years, from 1931 to 1944. During that period, El Salvador went through the first communist-led uprising in the Americas, a brief but determined attempt by a reform-minded political group to wrest power from the landowning oligarchy that had governed the country since 1871, and finally a reassertion of power by the old oligarchy backed by the United States, in the person of General Martinez. At a time when other countries were developing political and social institutions that would contribute to orderly national development in the future, El Salvador was ruled by a madman.

If one is to understand what is happening in El Salvador today, and is to try to fashion an intelligent policy to deal with these happenings, one must begin to understand the past of El Salvador. To understand the past is to come to the realization that El Salvador, in common with many other Latin American nations, had its moment when that society might have begun moving toward some type of orderly, institutionalized politics. Again in common with many other Latin American nations, that moment for El Salvador occurred in the late 1920s and early 1930s. Unfortunately for the nation, the moment passed with no progress being made in the direction of order and institutionalization. Rather, the oligarchy and the military, in the person of General Martinez, reasserted what was caudillistic control over the nation's economy, society, and politics, with the eventual unhappy results we are witnessing today.

In essence, all of the elements of this earlier period are present in El Salvador today. The spirit of Farabundo Martí, the great communist leader of the 1932 peasant revolt, is much in evidence among the guerrilla organizations, and the government today continues the brutal policies introduced in the 1930s. One of the leading right-wing death squads is named after General Martinez. Quite possibly, the root cause of the warfare is the simple fact that the people of that country simply will no longer stand meekly by while a brutal military, out of control, murders, rapes, and pillages defenseless civilians. At the same time, however, it must be realized that El Salvador is a country with literally no real political parties (with the possible exception of the Christian Democrats) and few political institutions worth mentioning. Instead, it is and has been a country governed by a few individuals with the power to force their will on others. If Argentina in the 1970s approached Hobbes' state of nature, El Salvador in the 1980s is Hobbes state of nature, with its war of all against all. How, exactly, did it get that way?

The Environment

In the 1920s El Salvador, in common with many other Latin American nations, began to undergo an awakening of democratic spirit that threatened to wash away the last bulwarks of the oligarchical rule that the country had experienced since 1871. Nascent political organizations sprang up, and more and more adult males began to participate in the electoral process, as if it were somehow meaningful. The Salvadoran oligarchy had always legitimized its rule through elections, which were always managed so that the candidate of the oligarchy won. By the 1920s however, this type of legitimizing process had become more and more risky, as new groups began to enter the political system; and new leaders, some challenging the system directly, began to appear on the scene. A major reason for these changes was undoubtedly the uprising by Augusto Sandino in Nicaragua against continued occupation of that country by U.S. Marines. Sandino became a heroic figure for many Central Americans of the time, and one in particular, a young Salvadoran named Farabundo Marti, actually went to Nicaragua to fight alongside the Nicaraguan hero.[1] Of course, societal changes, just beginning in El Salvador, also were causing some of the political changes. El Salvador had been one of the most overpopulated countries in the world, and by the 1920's this popula-

tion pressure was becoming more acute. One result of
this was extraordinarily good communications linking all
areas of the country with every other area. There is no
such thing as a "typical" Latin American country, and El
Salvador proves the adage. In El Salvador unlike most
other Latin American nations, the distinction between
urban and rural areas was never great. Communications,
literacy, schools, and the like spread to the countryside in El Salvador as rapidly as they appeared in the
capital, with the result that the peasants became more
highly socially mobilized much earlier in that country
than they did in neighboring Guatemala, for example.

A third major reason for political change during
the 1920s in El Salvador was the rise of labor and other
organizations. As early as 1917, the so-called Liga
Roja (Red League) was founded by the brother-in-law of
President Melendez. It was, in fact, merely a vehicle
to propel its founder into the presidency in 1923, in
perpetuation of what then appeared to be a Melendez
family dynasty. Other, more serious organizations
sprang up, including the Socorro Rojo Internacional,
founded by Farabundo Marti in the late 1920s. This
organization used propaganda to the rural workers as a
means to its ends, which were to smash the power of the
ruling oligarchy and substitute its own vision of
Salvadoran society in its place.

All of the above should not, however, convey a
picture of a nation moving rapidly into the age of mass
society. Such was definitely not the case. El
Salvador, along with most of Central America, remained
on the fringes of the great movements of the early
twentieth century that were being felt with greater
force in the larger countries of Latin America. On the
other hand, El Salvador did have a history during this
period, and it was related to succeeding events in that
country. It is inaccurate to state, as does one historian, that "Rule by a few wealthy families was usual from
the late nineteenth century until 1931, when the country
fell under the rule of General Maximiliano Hernandez
Martinez."[2] The country had a more convoluted
history, and changes in Salvadoran society in the post
World War I period were to have profound effects on subsequent events.

By 1927, the political dynasty founded in 1912 by
Carlos Melendez and continued through the early 1920s by
his brother and then his brother-in-law, had run its
course. Under the extra-official rules of Salvadoran
politics, the outgoing president was to pick his
successor, who would then be elected in a "democratic"
election. The outgoing President, unable to succeed
himself under the Salvadoran Constitution, picked as his
successor Don Pio Romero Bosque, a member in good
standing of the oligarchy, and a man who could, it was
thought, be trusted to continue the policies of his

predecessors. Don Pio didn't. Instead, he embarked
upon a mildly liberal-reformist course, culminating his
administration by throwing the 1931 presidential elections wide open for the first time in memory. Part of
the reason for Romero's action lay with the machinations
of two young firebrands, Juan Fernandez Anaya and
Agustin Farabundo Martí, both labeled (probably accu-
rately) as communists. Romero tried desperately during
his four years in office to walk the narrow line between
repression and permissiveness, alternately jailing the
two young revolutionaries and trying at the same time to
undercut their programs with reforms of his own. Free
elections, which fit in with Don Pio's own political
philosophy, seemed to be just the thing to stem the
rising tide of discontent fanned by Anaya and Marti.

The elections of 1931 were the freest El Salvador
had experienced in the twentieth century:

> Unfortunately, since such an election had never
> been held before, there was absolutely no mach-
> inery of democracy in operation. There was no
> two-party system; indeed, there was no real
> party system at all, but simply a number of
> caudillos, local chieftains supported by their
> own followers. There were no party primaries,
> no screening of candidates. The result was a
> reasonably free, but very chaotic, election.[3]

Of the several candidates in the election, only Don
Arturo Araujo received the backing of the rapidly growing labor movement in the rural areas of the country.
Araujo was a rich landowner from the northeast area of
the country, who had exhibited vaguely liberal creden-
tials at times during his life, much of which had been
spent abroad. Other candidates represented various
conservative elements in the country, with the exception of General Maximiliano Hernandez Martinez, who was
an unknown quantity at the time. The General had
entered the race on May 28, after resigning his position
as Inspector-General of the Army. Martinez made few
speeches and offered few concrete proposals during his
abbreviated campaign. Two days before the election was
due to begin (it was to be a three-day affair) in
January, 1931, Martinez mysteriously dropped out of the
race in favor of Araujo, who proceeded to win approximately forty-eight percent of the votes cast. In spite
of what was a resounding victory in a five-man field,
Araujo's failure to achieve an absolute majority meant
that the election was thrown into the legislature, which
duly declared him the winner in early February.

Despite the tremendous economic problems caused by
the Great Depression for the Salvadoran economy, as of
early 1931 the prospects for orderly democratic development looked brighter in El Salvador than they did in

many other Latin American countries:

> In the elections of January, 1931, the people
> had overwhelmingly chosen Don Arturo Araujo.
> Their choice had been duly ratified by the
> legislature when it unanimously chose him
> president. Despite the problems of the depres-
> sion it was expected that his regime would
> accomplish great things. He represented a new
> dawning of democracy in a coup-ridden country,
> scientific expertise in a land where lawyers
> and colonels usually ruled. He was a cosmo-
> politan in a nation noted for its provin-
> cialism.[4]

As it turned out, however, the elation felt by many
at the time was to be short-lived. The new president
was in an almost untenable situation. Faced with
implacable hostility from the right, he attempted with
little success to placate the left. There simply was
not enough money nor expertise in the government to move
toward social reform as fast as the growing leftist
groups demanded. On the right the conservatives, stung
by the election and fearful of losing their perquisites
to people they considered sub-human refused to participate in the government, thereby depriving it of the only
major fund of expertise in the country. All the while,
coffee prices continued to fall, as the depression hit
harder at the country's major foreign exchange earner.
Faced with a deteriorating situation, Araujo began to
lean more and more on General Martinez, who was now both
Minister of War and Vice-President of the Republic.
    The deteriorating situation ultimately produced a
military coup, headed by a group of junior army
officers, in the early hours of December 2, 1931. The
coup was successful, the President fled the capital and
later surrendered and went into exile, and within a few
days the coup leaders, in an attempt to gain recognition
from the United States, had named General Martinez as
provisional president, largely on the advice of the
U.S.'s chief Latin American trouble shooter, Jefferson
Caffery, who had flown to El Salvador from his post in
Bogota shortly after the revolt began.
    The policy of the United States toward the new
dictator was equivocal. On the one hand, the Department
of State refused to recognize Martinez, as he had vio-
lated the Washington Treaty of 1923, which prohibited
recognition of new governments coming to power through
force. On the other hand, U.S. business interests in El
Salvador, and the U.S. Mission there were arguing
Martinez's case through cables and visits to Washington.
In the end, faced with the alternatives of closing the
Mission or recognizing the new dictator, the Department
chose the expedient route and, on January 26, 1934,

recognized the government of General Maximiliano Hernandez Martinez as the legal government of El Salvador.[5]
What the course of Salvadoran history might have been
had the U.S. remained firm in its disapproval of the
dictatorship is open to conjecture.

For the next twelve years, however, El Salvador
endured a wild ride. Caffery, who had conspired against
the Revolution of 1933 in Cuba, had chosen to back a
most unusual dictator in El Salvador. Martinez's first
test as dictator came almost immediately after he
assumed office, as thousands of rural peasants, inspired
by Farabundo Marti, swept out of the mountains on
January 22, 1932, only to die by the thousands at the
hands of a Salvadoran army assured by its new leader
that it was fighting against a communist movement.[6]
Actually the revolt was a godsend for Martinez, as it
was instrumental in convincing both the local elite and
the United States that he was, perhaps, their only bul-
wark against communism in El Salvador. It has even been
suggested that the dictator planned the revolt and
instigated it with a two fold purpose: to gain support
from the U.S. and the local elite, and to eliminate
Marti and those leaders who might continue to oppose his
regime. By January 25, the revolt was over, Marti had
been captured and was to be put on trial, and the
killing of those who had participated in the revolt had
begun.[7] Martinez, who had obviously benefited from
the revolt and his role in ending it, now basked in the
approval of the Salvadoran elite.

The revolt had given him the excuse to declare a
state of siege, which now was to continue almost unin-
terruptedly throughout his regime. He was able to
default on his loans from the United States, thus
improving the economic situation of the country, simply
because money suddenly became less important when a true
anti-communist was on the scene:

> Again, in the case of the communist revolt,
> things simply broke his way. He could not
> order the communists to lead a revolt (although
> he did his best to annoy them at the time of
> the local elections), but he could only have
> been delighted that they proved foolish enough
> to revolt, and thus give him the opportunity to
> pose as the champion of law and order, not only
> to foreigners, but, more importantly, to the
> local wealthy class, whose support he desper-
> ately needed and was having a hard time
> winning.[8]

In the years after the revolt, a marriage of con-
venience existed between Martinez and the local
oligarchs. On the one hand, Martinez ruled with a free
(and iron) hand. On the other, he enjoyed the support

of the oligarchs, as he made no attempt to destroy their
privileged position within Salvadoran society. The relationship between Martinez and the oligarchs was but a
repetition of other such relationships throughout Latin
America. The dictator, who was not one of the elite,
served the purposes of the elite and therefore was
supported by them. The elite served the dictator's purposes by providing enough graft and political support to
enable him to function in office. The arrangement was
pure serendipity.

By early 1935, Martinez was securely in power,
having killed off his leftist opponents and having
gained the support of his friends on the right. For the
next nine years, El Salvador was governed as a thorough-
going police state. Martinez organized a political
party--the Partido Pro-Patria (Pro-Fatherland Party)--
which served to organize the elections of 1935 in which
Martinez's rule was legitimized in the traditional
Salvadoran way. The party reappeared as necessary when
"elections" were held again in 1938 and 1944, but
otherwise remained hidden from view.

World War II brought changes to Salvadoran society
that were not congenial to Martinez's rule. For one
thing, Martinez had predicated his government's policies
on restoring the coffee system to predominance in
Salvador, and in so doing had resisted industrialization. The War brought beginning industrialization to El
Salvador, and the dictator seemed suddenly out of step
with some of the new realities of Salvadoran society.
Moderate dissent finally crystallized around a
Salvadoran businessman named Arturo Romero, and a
general strike in 1944 succeeded in driving Martinez
from office. He fled to neighboring Honduras, where he
finally was murdered in 1966 by a workman on his
hacienda. The history of El Salvador after 1944, and
especially that of the last few years, is perhaps better
known. There was a short period of quasi-democracy,
coupled with intensive labor organization, followed by
the inevitable army coup and new dictatorships, none of
which were destined to last as long as that of General
Maximiliano Hernandez Martinez.

The Leader

Thus far, we have been concerned with political
personalities that have been considered more or less
"normal" in any typology of political types. When we
come face to face with General Martinez, however, we
begin to realize that the intermingling of private
personality and political action is a reality perhaps
greater than even Harold Lasswell would have us believe.
General Martinez was one of the strangest, if not the
strangest, Latin American leaders of the twentieth cen-

tury, and certainly belongs as a case study in Lasswell's Psychopathology and Politics.

There is no complete biography of Maximiliano Hernandez Martinez.[9] We do, however, know the basic facts of his early life, but these provide us with little or no insight into how and why he became the strange character who governed El Salvador. Maximiliano Hernandez Martinez was born in the town of San Matias, situated in the Department of La Libertad, on October 29, 1878. His parents were Raimundo Hernandez and Petrona Martinez, both of whom were farm workers. Both his parents were mestizos, and as far as we can tell, there was nothing to distinguish them from thousands of other parents of children born in El Salvador that year; except that young Maximiliano was not raised by his parents. Instead, most of his infancy was spent under the care of two aunts, Crecencia and Alejandra Martinez (perhaps the reason why he eventually was known by his matronym rather than his patronym, which is normal practice in El Salvador). Maximiliano spent his early years in school in the little neighboring town of Opico, walking back and forth from San Matias every day. As was the custom in El Salvador, an army patrol swept through the area picking up young men for military service, and Maximiliano was thus introduced rather forcibly to army life. After three years in the army, during which time Maximiliano completed grades four and five of primary school, he was released, and went to Guatemala to live with his uncle, who provided schooling for him through the bachillerato level. After this, the young man enrolled in the Escuela Politécnica Militar de Guatemala, or the Guatemalan equivalent of West Point. The Escuela is famous (or infamous) throughout Central America as providing the best and most reactionary military training available in the area. Many of the retrograde attitudes of the Guatemalan military can be traced to instruction at the Politécnica, as it is called. After graduating from Politécnica with the grade of Second Lieutenant, Martinez returned to El Salvador, where he entered the National University. After four years of study, Martinez left the University without his degree, and in 1902 entered the Salvadoran army as an officer. By 1919 Martinez had risen to the rank of General of Brigade in the Salvadoran army.

With the above biographical outline, it is difficult to ascertain why Martinez became the near-psychotic he was. Robert Coles and others might argue that the trauma of leaving his parents at such an early age might have set in motion the intellectual processes that produced the man who, when a smallpox epidemic was sweeping through El Salvador, ordered that the capital city of San Salvador be strung with colored lights to ward off the epidemic.[10] Martinez was a theosophist, who believed in the transmigration of human souls

from one body to another. He was quoted on one occasion
as stating that it was a greater sin to kill an ant than
a human being, as the soul of the ant could not trans-
migrate, while the human's soul could pass to a new
body.[11]

The General was fond of giving radio addresses to
his fellow citizens, to inform them of his views of the
world. On one occasion, he is reported as stating:

> It is good the children go barefoot. That way
> they can receive the beneficial effluvia of the
> planet, the vibrations of the earth. Plants
> and animals don't wear shoes.[12]

In another address:

> Biologists have discovered only five senses.
> But in reality there are ten. Hunger, thirst,
> procreation, urination, and bowel movements are
> the senses not included in the lists of the
> biologists.[13]

Perhaps the closest to a biography of Martinez is a
book by a former Salvadoran journalist, Alberto Peña
Kampy. Although the book in reality gives only a short
description of the General's early life and personal
habits, and is in the nature of a hagiography, the
following interesting information is included:

> It is known that General Martinez did not
> smoke, nor did he consume alcoholic beverages
> or drugs of any kind. His diet consisted
> solely of vegetables, and he ate no meat.
> Generally, he retired early at night and woke
> in the early morning....It is also known that
> General Martinez had the habit, after taking
> his bath and before eating breakfast, of drink-
> ing a glass of Pure Water that had been con-
> stantly exposed to the rays of the sun all the
> previous day in bottles of different colors,
> among them blue.
>
> From remote times it has been proved scienti-
> fically that ultra-violet rays, produced by the
> sun, contribute to the purification of pure
> water that is used especially for human
> nutrition.
>
> General Martinez, knowing about this, exposed
> to the rays of the sun, in a certain place on
> the roof of the building, bottles containing
> Drinking Water, without any other ingredient.
> These bottles were of different colors, among
> them the color blue, that produced what is

known scientifically as chromotherapy.[14]

The Area Handbook for El Salvador, an otherwise sober publication designed for military personnel and others who might be assigned to that country, put it this way:

> He (Martinez) kept bottles of colored water that he dispensed as cures for any disease, including cancer and heart trouble, and relied on complex magical formulas for the solution of national problems.[15]

This, then, was the man who governed El Salvador for thirteen years, from 1931 to 1944. To state that no political party development took place during this time is but to state the obvious.[16] The tragedy of El Salvador is very real to many people today. Some ascribe the problems there to the machinations of an international communist conspiracy which has seized upon that little country as its next target in its drive to conquer the world. Others see El Salvador's problems in a longer view, as stemming from the basic injustices of Salvadoran society and the brutality of the Salvadoran military over the years. A few see El Salvador as it really is--a society in which the most elemental parts of the social contract are missing and, in fact, have never been developed. El Salvador is ultimately untranslatable in normal political terms, which is a major continuing problem for the legions of earnest men and women who go down there attempting to implement some sort of United States policy in that unhappy country. In fact, novelists rather than political scientists seem to hold the key to understanding El Salvador. Joan Didion, in her book, Salvador, comes closest to describing a society that is largely undescribable in the jargon of the social sciences. Paul Theroux, in his book, The Old Patagonian Express, describes crowd behavior at a soccer game in San Salvador. His description offers insights into Salvadoran society worth ten thousand Area Handbooks. Finally, Gabriel García Marquez, in his book, the Autumn of the Patriarch, describes a mad dictator who governs a mythical country with a mixture of fear, magic, and death. In the book, the country and the dictator are mythical. After learning about the life and times of Maximiliano Hernandex Martinez, one comes to the conclusion that García Marquez does not write fiction after all. A major part of the tragedy of El Salvador today can be linked with the tragedy of rule by an insane man in an earlier epoch. We should not forget that the late twenties were a period of beginning growth of social and political institutions in El Salvador and that these modest beginnings were eliminated during the next thirteen years.

How different today's events might be if the mad
dictator described in the <u>Autumn of the Patriarch</u> had
not come to life in El Salvador from 1931 to 1944.

146

Notes

    1. Thomas P. Anderson, <u>Matanza: El Salvador's Communist Revolt of 1932</u>. (Lincoln, Nebraska: University of Nebraska Press, 1971), 34.
    2. Robert J. Shafer, <u>A History of Latin America</u>. (D.C. Heath and Company: Lexington, Massachusetts, 1978), 795.
    3. Anderson, 41.
    4. <u>Ibid</u>., 49.
    5. Kenneth J. Grieb, "The United States and The Rise of General Maximiliano Hernandez Martinez," <u>Journal of Latin American Studies</u>, III, 2. (Cambridge: University of Cambridge Press, 1971), 151-172.
    6. There is a great deal of conjecture over the exact amount of communist influence on the revolt. At the time of the initial Indian movement, Marti was in jail, and did not actually lead the Indians. Anderson's book, which is the only English account of the revolt and its aftermath, describes the situation in great detail.
    7. Estimates of those killed by government troops in the aftermath of the failed revolt range between 20,000 and 30,000. Marti and his fellow conspirators were tried by a military court and put to death by firing squad.
    8. Anderson, 146.
    9. The following brief facts concerning Martinez's life are taken from the following sources: Mari and Freddy Leistenschneider, <u>Gobernantes de El Salvador</u> (San Salvador: Imprenta Nacional, 1980); Alberto Peña Kampy, <u>El General Martinez: Un Patriarcal President Dictator</u> (San Salvador: Editorial Tipografía, 1972); John Baily et. al., <u>El Salvador de 1840 a 1935</u> (San Salvador: UCA/ Editores, 1978); Anderson; Joan Didion, <u>Salvador</u> (New York: Simon and Schuster, 1983); John D. Martz, <u>Central America: The Crisis and the Challenge Area Handbook for El Salvador</u>.
    10. Didion, 54.
    11. Martz.
    12. Didion, 53-54.
    13. <u>Ibid</u>.
    14. Pena, 37.
    15. United States, Department of Defense, <u>Area Handbook for El Salvador</u> (Washington, D.C.: USGPO, 1971).
    16. Alastair White, <u>El Salvador</u> (London: Ernest Benn Limited, 1973), 101. "It remained Martinez's policy throughout the rest of his Presidency to prevent any political activity by advocates of structural reform."

10
Political Leaders
and Political Parties

The relationship between the political actor and his environment is not new. Yet, it took Harold Lasswell, writing in the early 1930s, to remind us that "History without biography is a form of taxidermy." Since that time, a number of writers have emphasized the importance of the political actor within a particular political milieu. This work has been, in part, a reaffirmation of this theme: political actors do, depending upon their dispensability within the particular political situation, affect the outcome of political situations to a greater or lesser degree.

A second basic idea with which this work has grappled has been the idea of political personality, particularly the political personality of leaders. It took the herculean labor of James McGregor Burns to remind us of the importance of leadership in determining political outcomes, and, more importantly, how different types of political leadership personality might be formed. Finally, Burns and others advance the idea that different types of leadership personality might produce widely varying outcomes in certain political situations. In the context of the political party Burns identified the successful leader as one who was a "transactional" leader, that is, one who is willing to make deals and engage in bargaining in order to lead. Burns and others have attempted to examine the wellsprings of this and other types of political leadership through the lives of some famous (and infamous) leaders. This also has been a theme of this work.

This work breaks new ground by dealing explicitly with the leadership factor in the creation, development, and decay of political parties in the Third World, specifically Latin America. What roles have leaders played in the birth, growth, and death of political parties in Latin America, and what leaders have succeeded and why have they succeeded? Who have the failures been, and why have they failed? It has been suggested, further, that the existence of institutionalized political parties is a vital, if not essential, element in the attainment of a modicum of non-authoritarian stability in Latin America. This book corroborates earlier findings of a strong relationship between the existence of institutionalized political parties and a relative absence of violence and repression in certain societies, and provides the historical insight necessary to confirm a quantitative relationship. We now have two different types of evidence that strong political parties are an integral part of political peace and democractic development in Latin America. When one looks around the hemisphere, or around the world, today, the importance of this evidence for the future lives of the 3 billion inhabitants of the Third World cannot be overestimated. If these people are to live their lives without the daily (and nightly) fear of the dictatorship, then the development of political parties must proceed apace. In nations where this has not happened, we find a bloody tyrant, civil strife, or both. Thus, the long shadow of Yrigoyen looms over the Argentine political landscape. The utterly insane dictatorship of Maximiliano Hernandez Martinez influences events in El Salvador, even as our government attempts short-term solutions to long-range problems. The Sendero Luminoso terrorists in Peru are a direct result of the joint failure of that country's elite and the leaders of APRA to bring that party to political power. Latin America is, and always has been, an area of extreme diversity and of political and social anomalies, and for those reasons we do not want to become too deterministic in our theorizing. There are, of course, many factors other than political parties at work in the cauldron of Latin American politics, some rational and others apparently irrational to North American social scientists. In a real sense, Gabriel García Marquez can teach us more about Latin American politics than legions of gringo political scientists. Nevertheless, wherever one looks in Latin America, the political party seems to be an important political variable, and a study of its development and decay in various nations of the hemisphere should be instructive. Further, an examination of the lives of those leaders associated with the development and decay, with success and failure, in political party histories, should provide not only an understanding of past and present events, but also some insight into the possible future.

   Although recent efforts within the social sciences have generally tended to obscure the face, the effect of political actors upon political outcomes has long been a theme of historians and social scientists alike. What has been missing, usually, has been any real sense of discrimination--that is, how much effect did a particular personality have upon a discrete situation in which he was involved? We have, fortunately, come a long way from Carlisle and his "Great Man" theory of history, and

even from Sidney Hook's idea of the "Hero In History."
Fred Greenstein and others have provided us with more
discriminating measures of actor influence. Even though
we cannot meet the exacting criteria of some of our
colleagues, and provide precise quantitative measures of
the degree of influence, we can now rank the degree of
"actor dispensability" in a given situation, based upon
an examination of the historical situation and the
actions taken by a particular individual in that situation. For example, we can, based upon our examination
of the previous chapters, conclude that Hipólito
Yrigoyen in Argentina had a great deal more influence
over the political outcome in that nation than did, say,
Grau San Martín in Cuba a few years later. Briefly put,
Grau had much less freedom of political maneuver during
his tenure in office in 1933 than did Yrigoyen in
Argentina in the 1920s. In Cuba, environmental factors
weighed more heavily on the eventual outcome than they
did in Argentina. Grau simply did not control the
situation to the extent that Yrigoyen did. Other
factors, including the power of the United States to
control events on the island, the attitude of U.S.
Emissaries, and the machinations of the Cuban military,
led by Fulgencio Batista, all conspired to place Grau
high on any index of actor dispensability. Compared to
Grau, Yrigoyen was not nearly as constrained in his
choices by environmental factors, and therefore would
rank low on the same index. Similarily, Trujillo in the
Dominican Republic, Alessandri in Chile, and Calles in
Mexico all would rank relatively close to Yrigoyen on
the index; while Hernandez Martinez in El Salvador,
Betancourt in Venezuela, and Haya de la Torre in Peru
would all rank in the middle of the index, as indicated
in Figure 2.

Through the process of historical inquiry into
certain discrete situations, we can begin to verify
empirically Greenstein's idea of actor dispensability;
for it is a fact that each of the political actors we
have studied has had either more or less freedom of
action, depending on the environment in which he operated. While we cannot be statistically exact in our

Grau San Martin	Hernandez Martinez Betancourt Haya de la Torre	Yrigoyen Trujillo Calles Alessandri
Actor Dispensable		Actor Indispensable

Figure 2

measurements, we can begin to discriminate among various actors and various situations, which should lead to a greater appreciation of the intricate mix of personality and environment that ultimately produces political outcomes.

Implicit in the idea of actor dispensability is, of course, the idea of political personality. Trujillo was indispensable in the Dominican Republic precisely because only someone with his political and administrative gifts, perverted as they were, could have so completely dominated the political situation of that country for so long. Put another way, Grau San Martin, in the same situation in the same country, would still have ranked close to the actor dispensable side of the continuum. So there is an interplay between the idea of the varying influence of the political actor and the personality of that actor. Generally, those actors with greater charisma tend to control situations to a greater degree than those with less charisma. Certainly, the two most charismatic leaders we have studied, Yrigoyen and Alessandri, both were relatively indispensable largely because of their undisputed charismatic appeal to the masses of their countries. Trujillo's rather peculiar political gifts of cunning, hard work, and ferocity did not translate into a charismatic appeal, but he is, perhaps, an exception to most rules of politics in Latin America, as well as this one.

On the other side of the index, we can see that charismatic leaders are not always indispensable. Certainly, Haya de la Torre, especially in his earlier days, exerted a strong charismatic appeal to many Peruvians (although this may have been somewhat overstated by his North American admirers). Nevertheless, strong environmental factors conspired to limit the role this charismatic leader played in the political outcome of his country. Grau, beset by enormous environmental obstacles and lacking a great deal of personal charisma, influenced events in Cuba even less than did Haya de la Torre in Peru.

What about the actors in the middle? Interestingly, none of the three we have studied possessed any real charisma, in the sense of emotional appeals to the masses. Calles probably took the step of creating the PNR precisely because he lacked the charismatic appeal that would have permitted him to assume the role of the caudillo, while Betancourt concentrated on political organization in part to offset his lack of charismatic appeal to his fellow Venezuelans. Martinez, of course, remains almost an enigma. Certainly, selling water in blue bottles to cure dysentery does not constitute charisma, even in El Salvador in the 1930s. Whatever his peculiar political gifts were, Martinez does not leap out of the pages of the history books as do some of his contemporaries: Ubico in Guatemala, the early

Somoza in Nicaragua, or Carias Andino in Honduras.
   What all of the above suggests is that there is
some relationship between charisma and actor dispensability, but that, depending on the importance of the
environmental conditions surrounding the particular
political event, this relationship may be more or less
muted and obscured. We thus have an interplay of three
variables: political personality (measured by
charisma), actor dispensability, and the effect of
environmental variables, both endogenous and exogenous,
on the event. While all of these must be taken into
account in assessing any political event, the individual
actor and the political personality of that actor are
important factors in determining political outcomes.
   Burns defines a transactional leader as one who
approaches his "...followers with any eye to exchanging
one thing for another; jobs for votes or subsidies for
campaign contributions."[1] Transactional leadership
is, to Burns, one of two basic types of leadership, the
other being transformational, in which the leader
"...converts followers into leaders and may convert
leaders into moral agents."[2] While Burns' definitions
do not exactly fit our purposes, it is obvious that the
type of leader best-suited to build political institutions is the transactional leader, which is really
another name for the politician--the person who will
make deals and who attempts to manipulate institutions
to serve his power needs, rather than making emotional
appeals to the masses. Certainly, a major premise of
this study has been to confirm Burns' view of the transactional leader as identified with political parties.
We have, however, gone a step beyond, and have shown
that the transactional leader--the leader sans
charisma--is vital to the creation and development of
political parties in Latin America. Conversely, we have
shown that the transformational, or charismatic, leader
has consistently failed to develop these political
institutions in Latin America. We may, in fact, go
further and state that the transformational leader has
usually been a negative influence in institution-
building in Latin America. Once again, our case studies
demonstrate the point. Two of the greatest failures in
Latin American political history--Alessandri and
Yrigoyen--were both transformational leaders. Both men
engaged in leadership which was "...dynamic leadership
in the sense that the leaders throw themselves into a
relationship with followers who will feel 'elevated' by
it and often become more active themselves, thereby
creating new leaders."[3] Interestingly, Burns' char-
acterization of transformational leadership, especially
his sub-category of heroic leadership, in which the
transformational leader becomes "...motivated by powerful needs for affection, esteem, and self-actualiza-

tion"[4] dovetails neatly with Lasswell's description of the political agitator, whose essential mark is "the high value he places on the emotional response of the public."[5] The agitators, or heroic leaders,

> ...when landed in responsible posts, long to desert the official swivel for the roving freedom of the platform and the press. They glorify men of outspoken zeal, men who harry the dragons and stir the public conscience by exhortation, reiteration, and vituperation.[6]

Quite obviously the agitator, or transformational leader, has his place in the political process. He appears most often at times of national crisis, and his ability to inspire people to action may, at times, produce the most extraordinary political results. One thinks of the early Fidel Castro, Mao Zedong, and others who, by virtue of their political agitation swayed entire societies and altered the course of national, if not international histories. What they did not do, however, was to create institutions that outlasted their own considerable impact on their societies. They all suffered the same fate as Kwame Nkrumah, described by David Apter. In the end, Apter wrote, "Nkrumah lacked the imagination and skill to develop a country. He was a revolutionary without a plan—a visionary, but not a builder."[7] The development of institutions was left to others—Chou En-lai, Nehru, the Cuban Communist Party, or the Ghanaian military.
None of our leaders approached the prominence of the list above. However, our two political agitators, while not "pure" types, each approached the model of the political agitator. Each man came to power in a society undergoing a major systemic crisis brought on by the modernization process coupled with economic difficulties. Each tried to "solve" the problems of his society by direct personal action, without the intermediation of political and social institutions. Each had a vision, however clouded, of what "his" society should look like in the future, and each tended to divide the world into political friends and enemies. Dissent was taken as a sign of moral backwardness, and approval was equated with virtue. Each felt, ultimately, that he could overcome both personal and national problems by his own individual effort. In the case of both Yrigoyen and Alessandri, the individual's life trajectory had fortified that belief. Both had been born into middle-class families; both enjoyed privileged childhoods, in which other members of the family sacrificed to advance their education; and both enjoyed extraordinary early success in politics. There was no failure in either life until the final devastating and totally unexpected political calamity at the end of

their career. Not coincidentally, the life story of Victor Raul Haya de la Torre, our other quasi-agitator, follows the same line as those of Yrigoyen and Alessandri. It would appear that the Latin American middle-class is not the most fertile ground for institution-builders, especially when that class background is coupled with early, persistent, and rapid successes in politics.

The other type of political leadership, as presented by both Burns and Lasswell, is, in Burns' terms, transactional. We have already discussed Burns' definition of this type of leadership which Lasswell labels the political administrator. According to Lasswell, archetypal political administrators are

> ...those who have passed smoothly through their developmental crises. They have not overrepresented powerful hostilities, but either sublimated these drives, or expressed them boldly in the intimate circle. They display an impersonal interest in the task of organization itself, and assert themselves with firmness, though not with overemphasis, in professional and in intimate life....Their affects flow freely; they are not affectless, but affectively adjusted.[8]

It is almost as if Lasswell were describing our group of institution-builders: Calles, Betancourt, and Trujillo. Of the three, only Betancourt came from a middle-class family, and in his case there is scant evidence that his childhood was privileged at the expense of other family members. Both Calles and Trujillo had no chance at a privileged childhood: both were born into poor rural or semi-rural families. Calles' family situation was most uncertain, as he appears to have been handed from relative to relative during his early years. Calles was also the classic example of early failure leading to later success in institution-building. Calles' failures in business and in the military led to a realization of the limits of his ability to influence events through the force of his individual personality. Betancourt also knew failure, although his came later as he unsuccessfully battled an entrenched military and Venezuelan elite. Trujillo appears never to have prospered until he came to the attention of the Americans occupying the Dominican Republic, and they set him upon his course of domination over that nation. Each man experienced his developmental crises, and these in turn prepared him for the crucible of leadership to come. On the other hand, the agitators, at least in our study, seemed to have no major developmental crises or at least none of the magnitude experienced by the administrators. Let us

154

re-examine some individual cases in the light of the
generalizations set forth above.

In many ways, Plutarco Calles was the most successful institution-builder in Latin American history.
Certainly his institution, the PRI, has succeeded in
controlling the politics of that country for a longer
period of time and more completely than any of the other
political institutions we have surveyed. While we
admittedly do not know as much about Calles' early life
as we would wish, it seems clear that he was presented,
early on, with the overwhelming crisis of being poor in
a poor society. Not only was he poor; he also may have
been illegitimate. At the least, he had no station in
the society of the small towns in which he lived during
his early years. Further, these were towns far away
from the centers of power in Mexico, and this too
contributed to a sense of powerlessness and a feeling
that the individual, through his own efforts, could
accomplish little in life. Contrast this childhood and
early adulthood with that of Yrigoyen, Haya, or
Alessandri, and Calles' sense of personal impotence, of
lack of control over events, can perhaps be better
appreciated. For, in contradistinction to Calles, each
of these three future leaders experienced a great deal
of personal accomplishment in his early years, and the
resultant accompanying sense of personal power that went
with that success. Further, they were, at an early age,
near the center of things. Yrigoyen was born into an
intensely political family in Buenos Aires; while both
Alessandri and Haya migrated to the capital from
relatively important regional centers early in their
life. Calles, by contrast, remained in the Mexican
northwest until he was in his mid-thrities, and then
migrated to Mexico City only on the heels of his hero
and patron, Alvaro Obregon. Rafael Trujillo also faced
the overpowering obstacle in his youth of being poor and
rural in a poor nation. Further, he remained in the
hinterland until later in life. Of the three administrators, only Romulo Betancourt migrated to the city
during his youth. However, once there, Betancourt
failed to achieve the success experienced by Yrigoyen,
Haya, or Alessandri. Betancourt was always overshadowed
by more illustrious figures during his student days,
while the nature of the Venezuelan political and social
system made easy success for Betancourt even more
unlikely.

It seems almost paradoxical to state that military
men appear to be the best builders of political institutions in Latin America, but at least the case studies in
this work indicate that they are. Both Calles and Trujillo were abject failures until they found the military
vocation, and both retained their ties with the military
throughout their lives--Trujillo openly as an army
General, and Calles more tangentially, first as Minister

of Defense under Obregón, then as President (Calles'
initial institutionalization of the Mexican army may
have been his greatest political feat), and then as a
sort of unofficial Jefe Supremo of the armed forces.
Perhaps, in retrospect, the seeming paradox is not there
after all. The military appears to have provided both
Calles and Trujillo with important elements for their
later political success. First, it provided both men
with a vehicle for their true talents, which had not
prospered before. In the case of Calles, his skill at
organization came to the fore only after he joined
forces with the Mexican Revolution. Calles was never a
military genius, as was his friend Obregon. He was,
however, someone who could organize men and materials,
and in the context of the revolutionary years from 1910
to 1917, this skill was sorely needed. Trujillo's
organizational skills also came to the fore in the
military. Further, his lust for power, which had either
been thwarted or sublimated during his earlier civilian
existence, could now be unharnessed. The military also
trained both Calles and Trujillo further in the art of
organization and administration. For the army is
essentially a bureaucracy, and it rewards administrators
as well or better than it does the military genius.
Finally, the military provided each future leader with a
way out of his poverty and obscurity. The military does
not often do this, as in most instances the talents
necessary for success within the military are not in
evidence in young men with Calles' and Trujillo's
backgrounds. Normally, it is the middle-class youth who
make it to the top of the military ladder in Latin
America, rather than the sons of the rural poor. In the
two case studies, however, the military played a key
role in providing both opportunity and training for the
future political leader.

     Of course, while the military in the Dominican
Republic and in Mexico were providing opportunities for
Calles and Trujillo, the military in El Salvador was
creating a very different type of political leader in
General Martinez. Why the difference in final outcome?
We can only surmise, as we still do not have the biographical information on Martinez necessary for a full
explanation. It appears, however, that Martinez did not
have the same type of childhood as Calles and Trujillo.
Calles, even though he was not raised by his parents,
appeared to enjoy a warm relationship with his uncles
and aunts who were responsible for his upbringing.
Trujillo, on the other hand, was reared in a family
atmosphere dominated by his mother, an extraordinary
woman who appeared capable of doling out love and discipline in equal quantitites. Both men, then, felt
wanted in a family environment, and each had a sense of
place within a limited environment. Martinez, on the
other hand, appears to have had neither. Raised first

by anonymous relatives, then by an uncle in Guatemala, sent to military school in Guatemala, and then conscripted into the Salvadoran army--there is no evidence that Martinez ever had a sense of belonging to a family, or of counting as a person to his own relatives. Given his background, it is eminently unsurprising that Martinez grew into adulthood as what might generously be called a borderline personality. Perhaps the most frightening aspect of this study is the realization that Martinez's childhood is being replicated millions of times throughout Latin America and that his young life, not that of Calles, Betancourt, or Trujillo, is the norm among the poor of Latin America.[9]

What effect does education have upon the political personality of Latin American leaders? Trujillo and Calles had little, if any, formal education, even though Calles claimed to have been a school teacher at one time. Martinez graduated from the Guatemalan Politécnica, oftentimes called the Guatemalan West Point. In actuality, the Politécnica provides a much narrower education and outlook, and the educational level is not much higher than many secondary military schools in the United States.[10] Betancourt, Alessandri, and Haya all had university educations, with the former two receiving their licenciados, while Haya appears never to have graduated from San Marcos. Yrigoyen received a degree in Law from the University of Buenos Aires. Grau San Martín was the best educated of the group, with an MD degree from the University of Havana and further study in France.

One may only surmise as to the effect that education has on political personality, and the effect probably varies from society to society. Generalizing: in societies like those of Latin America, where only a small number of people go beyond a basic elementary education, a person who is highly educated may understandably feel that he has a special place in that society. Certainly, many university-educated Latin American youth do have this feeling. In fact, of course, they are the educational elite of their societies much more than college-educated youth are in the United States. Further, in a society where a college degree is still a scarce commodity, that scarce commodity will be prized more than in a society in which larger percentages of college-age youth have that degree. Finally, the type of education received by those who attended the university was of the classical variety. In this type of education, ideas are valued above systems, the worth and importance of the individual is stressed; even though there is a concomitant Marxist approach to history and events. Thus, the individual, not the institution, becomes important in explaining past events, and, by inference, the individual will control future events as well. Those who lack this type of education may be more prone to accept institutions as major predictors of political outcomes, and may be more disposed to work for and through those institutions as part of their political personality.

What emerges, then, are two syndromes associated with each of our two major types of political personality. The political agitator tends to come from a certain background, while the administrator tends to emerge from a distinct environment. It should be emphasized at this point, lest the reader think we are totally deterministic, that these appear as tendencies only. Politics, as is all of life, is still too chaotic, too much a product of chance, for us to draw any hard and fast lessons from our case studies. Yet, the tendencies are there, as indicated below:

Figure 3

	Agitator	Administrator
Economic background	Middle to upper class	Poor to middle class
Family background	Favored within family, family lineage important	Family unknown or without lineage, family atmosphere accepting but discipline apparent
Geographical location	Urban, either at birth or in early years	Rural in early years at least
Occupation	Lawyer, Medical Doctor, Professional politician	Military, professional politician
Education	University	Grade school or less

This work has been conceived of partly as a corrective to an overemphasis within the social sciences on so-called "environmental" factors. For this reason, and because so little work has been done on the importance of political leadership in determining political outcomes in Latin America, we have tended to concentrate on the political actor. However, as the case studies have hopefully made clear, each political actor works within and is constrained by his political environment. Now, "environment" is one of those catch-all words within the social sciences that generally means everything other than the thing the author is concentrating on, and we have perhaps been guilty of using the word in this slipshod manner throughout the case studies. Let us now be more specific. By environment we mean all of those

variables which, taken together, form the constraints
and opportunities for the political actor. Environmental factors may be domestic or foreign. They may be
economic, social, or none of the above. The triumph of
the Brazilian futbol team in the World Cup in 1968
undoubtedly provided a more favorable environment, at
least temporarily, for the Brazilian generals who had
assumed governance of the country in 1964. The
generals, especially Costa e Silva, were able to identify their regime with Brazil's sporting success, thereby
gaining at least temporary public approval of their
regime. Similarly, the environment includes foreign as
well as domestic factors. The role of the United States
in the Cuban situation in 1933 has been covered in our
study of Grau San Martin. Obviously, Grau would have
had a much greater chance for political success had the
United States not been unalterably opposed to his administration, and had not Jefferson Caffery personally
disliked Grau. Many times, the effects of the foreign
environment are not so easily discernible. The so-
called "demonstration effect," whereby people in Latin
America choose to emulate the folkways of the United
States, or the political and economic theories of Karl
Marx, have a profound and not easily understood effect
on the politics of those countries. It is difficult,
for example, to determine the spillover of the effects
of United States low culture (the McDonald's syndrome)
into political attitudes. That there is some spillover
is indisputable, but exactly how much and in what
direction is a matter of some dispute. Yet, the
environment, both domestic and foreign, most certainly
provides the background, the necessary but not determining conditions, within which the political actors
operate. Sometimes, as we have indicated, the environment is more determining, more overwhelming in its
effects, than in others. Even if he had had a strong
administrative personality, it is doubtful that Grau
would have succeeded in fashioning a permanent political
organization in Cuba in 1933. The predominant factor in
that situation was the attitude of the United States.
        To a lesser degree, Yrigoyen in Argentina and
Alessandri in Chile were victims of the world depression
of the early 1930s. They had enjoyed great success
during the heady economic climate of the 1920s, but
their one-man political acts could not survive the
sudden economic downturns that occurred in both
Argentina and Chile. Sometimes other political actors
constitute a major part of the environment. Without
Farbundo Marti and the campesino uprising in El Salvador
in 1932, it is doubtful that Martinez would have been
able to consolidate his political power over the next
twelve years. Certainly, he would not have achieved the
approval of both the local elite and the United States
as easily, had he not suddenly appeared as the anti-

communist champion in El Salvador. At other times the
very nature of the society in which the political actor
operates can be an important factor in determining the
environment. The basically authoritarian nature of the
society of the Dominican Republic certainly made
Trujillo's task of ruling much easier than it would have
been in Mexico, with its recent legacy of a great social
revolution.

The environment, then, is composed of many different factors, many of which may not appear to have any
overtly political significance at first glance. Nevertheless, if we stretch the word "social" to include six-
day bike races and the like, we can state that the
environment is usually composed of economic, social, and
other-actor factors, both domestic and foreign.
Further, while we once again cannot measure the
environment in a strict quantitative sense, we can
differentiate among favorable and unfavorable
environments in a comparative sense. We can, for
instance, point out that the Cuban environment in 1933
was more unfavorable for the development of political
institutions than was the case in any other situation we
have examined. This unfavorable environment was composed of the negative attitude of the United States, the
machinations of elements of the Cuban military, led by
Fulgencio Batista, and the general downturn in the Cuban
economy caused by the Great Depression. Next, the Peruvian and Salvadoran environments were also unfavorable
for institutional development, for differing reasons.
In Peru, the environment was overwhelmingly domestic in
origin, and consisted of the antideluvian attitudes of
the Peruvian military and the elite toward granting
participation in the political system to those currently
outside that system. A further telling component of the
Peruvian environment was the passivity or indifference
of the Indians toward APRA, a movement ostensibly
designed to bring them political and economic benefits.
In El Salvador, a major part of the environment was the
history of the country, with its recurring coups,
political instability, and authoritarian leaders. The
attitude of the Salvadoran elite toward political
change--fearing it--also contributed to an environment
unconducive to political institutionalization. Finally,
the activities of Farabundo Marti, which resulted in
raising the spectre of communism just as it appeared
that General Martinez might not last in office, contributed greatly to his subsequent political longevity.

Rómulo Betancourt in Venezuela also faced an unpromising political environment, also composed in large
part of the attitudes of both the military and the
ruling class toward democratic evolution. In many ways,
perhaps the best comparative study of the impact of personality on political outcomes might be a comparison of
Victor Raul Haya de la Torre in Peru and Rómulo Betan-

court in Venezuela. Both men faced unpromising political environments, in which those who ruled and who had ruled the country since independence were unalterably opposed to the type of democratic evolution proposed by the two new political players. While the Peruvian oligarchy may have been more deeply entrenched, and Peru less susceptible to ideas from the outside world, the situation was remarkably similar in the two countries. Yet, in one, Betancourt stayed the course, organizing his party and exerting pressure for a democratic outcome. In the other Haya swung wildly from one extreme to another; at times espousing the democratic solution while at others plotting revolution, thereby confirming the oligarchy in their worst fears. For Betancourt, the end he struggled for was political power for his organization. For Haya, the end seemed much more confused, a combination of personal vainglory, ideological imperatives, and political power.

Finally, we come to the three most promising political environments in Latin America in the late 1920s, those in Argentina, Chile, and Mexico. These three nations, geographically, racially, and historically different, possessed political environments more conducive to the emergence of institutionalized poltical parties. In the case of Mexico, Jose Luis Reyna has already enumerated many of these factors: a rapidly growing electorate, fairly rapid urbanization, a changing social structure, and a lack of political institutions to represent these new groups. In addition, the traditional Mexican ruling elite--the oligarchy, to use that overworked word--had been destroyed by the Revolution of 1910, the first true social revolution to take place in post-independence Latin America.[11] The social and political situation was, in short, fluid, with no well-entrenched ruling class to overcome. The would-be innovators were, in fact, in power at the time. Finally, the Mexican economy, although it felt the effects of the world depression along with the rest of Latin America, was not prostrated by the world calamity.

The Chilean economy, on the other hand, was severely hit by the world depression, primarily because its exports were more vulnerable to belt-tightening in the northern nations than were those of Mexico. Nevertheless, there were in Chile counterbalancing factors, primarily the tradition of democracy in the country reaching back into the nineteenth century. In addition, Chile possessed one of the largest middle classes in Latin America at the time, a phenomenon that is supposed to encourage political institutionalization and democracy.[12] Further, the Chileans' image of themselves--sober, industrious, hardworking--should have contributed to further party development within a democratic framework. Finally, prior party development in

Chile meant that those who came along in the 1920s were building upon an edifice already begun in earlier times.

In Argentina, the political environment was, if anything, even more promising than in Mexico and Chile. Although the Argentine economy was hard hit by the world depression, the effects were less than those in Chile, and the Argentine internal economy, larger than that of Chile, was better able to withstand the drop in export earnings. Further, Argentina was a more "modern" nation than either Chile or Mexico. More of its people lived in cities, more were literate, health care and educational facilities were superior, and political information was more readily available to the general population. Finally, Argentina shared with Chile an equally long history of relatively free elections, political party development, and democratic political intercourse.

Here again, as in the case of Betancourt and Haya, we can discern the importance of the political actor. While no claims are made that the three environments described were exactly the same, the balance among the three was such that one might expect similar political outcomes in the three societies. Yet, of the three, only Mexico emerged with an institutionalized political party that would control events in that country for the next sixty years. These varying results were due, in large part, to the varying political personalities of three political actors. Each actor--Calles in Mexico, Alessandri in Chile, and Yrigoyen in Argentina--made decisions regarding the future of "his" political party based on a number of factors. The basic political personality of the leader--agitator or administrator, innovational or transactional--played a major role in determining those decisions. Yrigoyen and Alessandri, the agitators, chose to accrue power to themselves, at the expense of their political parties. Each man felt that he alone could control both the immediate and the long-range political destiny of both his party and his nation. Calles, the administrator, "knew" that he, as an individual, could not control the political future of Mexico. He therefore chose to construct an institution through which he might exert his control, both in the present and in the future. In fact, whether Calles was a statesman who foresaw the need for institutions to replace caudillos in Mexico, or whether he was an opportunistic politician who merely wanted to extend his control over the political system for a few more years, is largely beside the point. The important fact, for the future political stability of Mexico, was that Calles' political personality led him to attempt to work through political institutions rather than exert the force of his individual political prowess. At the other end of the continent, at about the same time, Yrigoyen and Alessandri chose to utilize their personal charisma

162

rather than to attempt to work through political institutions to resolve their political problems. The
subsequent political histories of Mexico, Argentina, and
Chile are in large part a result of these differing
political decisions, taken within remarkably similar
political environments, by political actors acting
largely on the basis of their political personalities.

Conclusion

The history of Latin America has often been written
almost solely in terms of great men: the
conquistadores, the liberators, the great caudillos of
the nineteenth and twentieth centuries. Unfortunately,
most of these individuals left little or no legacy in
the form of enduring institutions once they disappeared
from the scene. Indeed, a case could be made that the
curse of Latin American politics over the centuries has
been a lack of institution-builders and a plethora of
charismatic leaders. This book has tried to present a
more sophisticated view of Latin American political
leadership, by utilizing the concept of varying political personalities, and the different political outcomes
resulting from political actors possessing these
different attributes. We have tried to be faithful to
Harold Lasswell's dictum that "Political science without
biography is a form of taxidermy" without lapsing into a
simplistic "great man" theory of political development.
Through the various case studies, we have attempted to
demonstrate, in a rudimentary way, how historical biography might be used to explain the concept of varying
political personality, and what effect the differing
types of personality might have on political outcomes.
Further, we have attempted some corrective to both the
"great man" school of political history and the
completely sociological approach to the explanation of
political events. That there is an interaction between
the political actor and his environment cannot be
gainsaid, and the two must be considered together if any
meaningful explanations of political events are to be
forthcoming.
We have also attempted to resurrect an old theme,
but one that seems to be neglected more and more--the
idea that institutionalized political parties are a sine
qua non of political stability in Latin America and, by
inference at least, throughout the Third World. We are
not, in the process, stating that all institutionalized political parties are equally praiseworthy;
in fact, we have serious doubts about the basic political morality of the most institutionalized party in our
study, the Mexican PRI. Yet, just as we might prefer
Acción Democrática to the PRI on both moral and
aesthetic grounds, both are examples of the type of

political party seemingly essential to a modicum of
political peace. There are those who would argue that
this peace is bought at a terrible price, and that
revolution is the answer to the ills besetting Latin
American societies today. Perhaps so, but certainly the
argument can be made that life in Mexico or Venezuela is
superior in most respects and for most people to that in
Chile, El Salvador, or Cuba; to use three disparate
examples. Perhaps we are saying that the political
machine, with all its failings, is preferable to
rightist dicatorships, revolutionary situations, or
leftist dictatorships. Such has not been the intent of
this study, which has focused instead on the concept of
political personality, its effect upon political
actions, and the interrelationship of the political
actor and his environment. Nevertheless, when we consider the ideologues of this world, of both right and
left, the need for people who are "just politicians" and
the institutions they create becomes ever more apparent,
and ever more pressing if the nations of Latin America
are to evolve toward some form of democratic stability.

Notes

1. James McGregor Burns, Leadership (New York: Harper and Row, 1978), 336.
2. Ibid
3. Ibid., 337.
4. Ibid.
5. Harold Lasswell, Psychopathology and Politics (Chicago: University of Chicago Press, 1931), 75.
6. Ibid., 76
7. As quoted in Burns, 247.
8. Lasswell, 102.
9. See Carolina Maria de Jesus, Child of the Dark (New York, New American Library, 1964).
10. Richard N. Adams, Crucifixion By Power (Austin, TX: University of Texas Press, 1958), Chapter 4.
11. See Jean Meyer et.al., Historia de la Revolucion Mexicana (Mexico: El Colegio de Mexico, 1977), Volume I.
12. John J. Johnson, Political Change In Latin America: The Emergence of the Middle Sectors (Stanford, CA: Stanford University Press, 1958).

Bibliography

General

Aguilar, Luis. <u>Cuba: 1933</u>. Ithaca, NY: Cornell University Press, 1972.

Almond, Gabriel, and G. Bingham Powell. <u>Comparative Politics: A Developmental Approach</u>. Boston: Little, Brown, 1966.

Barber, James D. <u>The Presidential Character: Predicting Presidential Performance</u>. Englewood Cliffs: Prentice-Hall, 1977.

Benejam, Maria Antonieta, "Partido Revolucionario Institucional: Proceso de la Institucionalizacion de un Partido Politico." Unpublished thesis for licentiatura en Sociologia, Universidad Nacional Autonoma de Mexico, 1972.

Black, Cyril E. <u>The Dynamics of Modernization</u>. New York: Harper and Row, 1966.

Burns, James MacGregor. <u>Leadership</u>. New York: Harper and Row, 1978.

Crassweller, Robert. <u>Trujillo: Life and Times of a Caribbean Dictator</u>. New York: MacMillan, 1966.

Dahl, Robert. <u>Polyarchy, Participation, and Opposition</u>. New Haven: Yale University Press, 1971.

Duff, Ernest A. and John McCamant. <u>Violence and Repression in Latin America</u>. New York: The Free Press, 1976.

Duverger, Maurice. <u>Political Parties</u>. New York: John Wiley and Sons, 1963.

Dozer, Donald M. <u>Latin America: An Interpretive History</u>. New York: McGraw-Hill, 1962.

Erikson, Erik. <u>Young Man Luther</u>. New York: W. W. Norton, 1962.

Erikson, Erik. <u>Identity; Youth and Crisis</u>. New York: W. W. Norton, 1968.

Fagg, John E. <u>Latin America: A General History</u>. New York: MacMillan Publishing, 1977.

Greenstein, Fred, "The Impact of Personality on Politics: An Attempt to Clear Away the Underbrush,"

American Political Science Review 61 (1967).

Greenstein, Fred. _Personality and Politics_. New York: W. W. Norton, 1969.

Hofstadter, Richard. _The Idea of a Party System_. Berkeley: University of California Press, 1969.

Hook, Sidney. _The Hero in History_. New York: John Day, 1943.

Huntington, Samuel P. _Political Order in Changing Societies_. New Haven: Yale University Press, 1968.

Hermann, Margart G. and Thomas W. Milburn (eds). _A Psychological Examination of Political Leaders_, New York: Free Press, 1977.

Knowles, Henry P. _Personality and Leadership_. Reading, MA: Addison-Wesley Publishing Company, 1971.

Lasswell, Harold. _Psychopathology and Politics_. Chicago: University of Chicago Press, 1931.

LaPalombara, Joseph, and Myron Weiner. _Political Parties and Political Development_. Princeton: Princeton University Press, 1966.

Lawson, Kay. _The Comparative Study of Political Parties_. New York: St. Martin's Press, 1976.

Leiserson, Avery. _Parties and Party Politics_. New York: Alfred A. Knopf, 1958.

Lewis, Oscar. "The Culture of Poverty," _Scientific American_ 215:16 (October, 1966).

Lipset, Seymour Martin. _Political Man_. New York: Doubleday, 1960.

McDonald, Ronald H. _Party Systems and Elections in Latin America_. Chicago: Markham Publishing Co., 1971.

Martz, John D. _Acción Democrática_. Princeton: Princeton University Press, 1965.

Maslow, Abraham. _The Farther Reaches of Human Nature_. New York: The Viking Press, 1971.

Neumann, Sigmund (ed). _Modern Political Parties_. Chicago: University of Chicago Press, 1956.

Paige, Glenn D. _The Scientific Study of Political Leadership_. New York: Free Press, 1977.

Ruiz Massieu, Jose Francisco. _Normacion Constitucional de los Partidos Politicos en America Latina_. Mexico: Instituto de Investigaciones Jurídicas, 1974.

Rustow, Dankwart. _Philosophers and Kings_. New York: Braziller, 1970.

Sartori, Giovanni. _Parties and Party Systems_. New York: Cambridge University Press, 1976.

Scott, Robert E. _Mexican Government in Transition_. Urbana, Illinois: University of Illinois Press, 1964.

Szulc, Tad. _Twilight of the Tyrants_. New York: Praeger, 1959.

Thomas, Hugh. _Cuba: The Pursuit of Freedom_. New York: Harper and Row, 1971.

167

Toth, Michael. The Theory of the Two Charismas.
Washington D.C.: University Press of America, 1981.
Tsurutani, Taketsuga. The Politics of National Develop-
ment: Political Leadership in Transitional
Societies. New York: Chandler Publishing Co.,
1973.
Tucker, Robert C. Politics As Leadership. Columbia,
Missouri: University of Missouri Press, 1981.
Welsh, William A. "Methodological Problems in the Study
of Political Leadership in Latin America," Latin
American Research Review XI (Fall, 1978).

Mexico

Amaya, Juan Gualberto. Los Gobiernos de Obregon,
Calles, y Regimenes Peleles Derivados de Callismo,
Mexico City: Published by author, 1947.
Bailey, David C. Viva Cristo Rey! Austin: University
of Texas Press, 1974.
Benejam, Maria Antonieta. "Partido Revolucionario
Institucional; Proceso de Institucionalizacion de
un Partido Politico." Unpublished thesis for
Licenciatura en Sociologia, Facultad de Ciencias
Politicas y Sociales, Universidad Nacional Autonoma
de Mexico, 1972.
Blanco Moheno, Roberto. Crónica de la Revolucion
Mexicana: Tomo III; Vasconcelos, Calles, Cardenas.
Mexico City: Editorial Polis, 1949.
Bojorquez, Juan de Dios. Plutarco Elias Calles, Rasgos
Biograficos. Mexico City: PRI. Comision
Editorial, 1976.
Bremauntz, Alberto. Material Histórico de Obregón a
Calles. Mexico City: Avelar Hnos. Impresores,
1973.
Calles, Plutarco. "Presidential Papers." Mexico City:
Archivo General de la Nacion, various dates.
Carr, Parry. Organized Labour and the Mexican
Revolution: 1915-1928. Oxford: Latin American
Center, St. Anthony's College, Oxford University,
1972.
Casasola, Gustavo. Biografía Illustrada de General
Plutarco Elias Calles. Mexico City: n.p., 1975.
Chaverri Matamoros, Amado. El Verdadero Calles. Mexico
City: Editorial Patria, 1933.
Cuadros Caldas, Julio. El Comunismo Criollo. Puebla,
Mexico: n.p., 1930.
Gonzalez Casanova, Pablo. Democracy in Mexico. New
York: Oxford University Press, 1970.
Hansen, Roger D. La Politica del Desarrollo Mexican.
Mexico City: Siglo XXI Editores, 1967.
James, Daniel. Mexico and the Americans. New York:
MacMillan, 1963.
Kubli, Luciano. "Calles, El Hombre y su Gobierno."

168

Unpublished typescript in Archivo General de la
Nacion, Mexico City, n.d.

Lieuwen, Edwin. Mexican Militarism: The Political Rise
and Fall of the Revolutionary Army. Albuquerque:
University of New Mexico Press, 1968.

McCullagh, Francis. Red Mexico. New York: Wadsworth,
1929.

Medina, Fernando. Calles: Un Destino Melancólico.
Mexico City: Editorial Juz, 1960.

Meyer, Jean et. al. Historia de la Revolucion Mexicana,
Vol. XI, Estado y Sociedad con Calles. Mexico
City: El Colegio de Mexico, 1977.

Partido Nacional Revolucionario. La Democracia Social
en Mexico. Mexico City, 1929.

Partido Nacional Revolucionario. Memoria de la Segunda
Convencion Nacional del PNR. Mexico City, 1934.

Pihaloup, A. Gil. El General Calles y el Sindicalismo.
Mexico City: Herrero Hnos. y Sucesores, 1925.

Pereyra, Carlos. Mexico Falsificado: Tomo II. Mexico
City: Editorial Polis, 1949.

Portes Gil, Emilio. Quince Años de la Política
Mexicana. Mexico City: Ediciones Botas de Mexico,
1941.

Puente, Roman. Hombres de la Revolucion: Calles. Los
Angeles, CA: n.p., 1933.

Reyna, Jose Luis. "Movilizacion y Participacion
Politica," in Perfil de Mexico en 1980. Mexico
City: Universidad Nacional Autonoma de Mexico,
1976.

Rostow, Walt W. Stages of Economic Growth. New York:
Cambridge University Press, 1971.

Scott, Robert. Mexican Government in Transition.
Urbana, Illinois: University of Illinois Press,
1964.

Tannenbaum, Frank. Mexico, the Struggle for Peace and
Bread. New York: Alfred A. Knopf, 1951.

Watkins, Holland D. "Plutarco Calles." Unpublished PhD
Dissertation, Texas Technological University, 1968.

Wilkie, James W., and Edna Monzon de Wilkie. Mexico
Visto en el Siglo XX. Mexico City: Instituto
Mexicano de Investigaciones Economicas, 1969.

Zevada, Ricardo J. Calles El Presidente. Mexico City:
Editorial Nuestro Tiempo, 1977.

Dominican Republic

Atkins, G. Pope. Arms and Politics in the Dominican
Republic. Boulder, Colorado: Westview Press,
1981.

Crassweller, Robert D. Trujillo: Life and Times of a
Caribbean Dictator. New York: The MacMillan
Company, 1966.

Cripps, Louise L. The Spanish Caribbean: From Columbus

to Castro. Boston: G. K. Hall and Company, 1979.

o, Franklin J. Trujillismo: Genesis y Rehabilitacion. Santo Domingo: Editora Cultural Dominicana,
1971.

Galindez, Jesus de. The Era of Trujillo. Tucson,
Arizona: The University of Arizona Press, 1973.

Gutierrez, Carlos Maria. El Experimento Dominicano.
Mexico: Editorial Diogenes SA, 1974.

Hicks, Albert C. Blood in the Streets. New York:
Creative Age Press, 1946.

Jimenez, R. Emilio. Biografía de Trujillo. Ciudad
Trujillo: Editorial Caribe, 1955.

Nanita, Abelardo R. Trujillo. Ciudad Trujillo:
Editorial del Caribe, 1954.

Ornes, German E. Trujillo: Little Caesar of the
Caribbean. New York: Thomas Nelson and Sons,
1958.

Perez Cabral, Pedro Andres. La Communidad Mulata.
Caracas: Grafica Americana, 1967.

Rodman, Selden. Quisqueya: A History of the Dominican
Republic. Seattle: University of Washington
Press, 1964.

Thomson, Charles A. Dictatorship in the Dominican
Republic. New York: Foreign Policy Association,
1936.

Trujillo Molina, Rafael L. Discursos, Mensajes, y
Proclamas. Santiago, Dominican Republic: 1946,
Editorial El Diario (11 volumes).

Trujillo Molina, Rafael L. Fundamentos y Políticas de
Un Regimen. Ciudad Trujillo, Dominican Republic:
Editora del Caribe, 1960.

Trujillo Molina, Rafael L. Discursos, Mensajes, y
Proclamas. Madrid: Ediciones Aries, 1957.

Wiarda, Howard J. The Dominican Republic: Nation in
Transition. New York: Frederick A. Praeger, 1969.

Venezuela

Abascal, Arturo Sosa. Del Garibaldismo Estudiantil a la
Izquierda Criolla: los Origenes Marxistas del
Proyecto de A.D. Caracas: Ed. Centauro, 1981.

Acción Democrática. Secretaria Nacional de Propaganda.
Acción Democrática: Doctrina y Programa. Caracas:
Secretaria Nacional de Propaganda, 1962.

Acción Democrática, Secretaria Nacional de Prensa y
Propaganda. Ratificacion de Principios Teoricos y
de Orientacion Programatica Normativos de Accion
Democratica. Caracas: Secretaria Nacional de
Prensa y Propaganda, 1958.

Alexander, Robert J. Rómulo Betancourt and the Transformation of Venezuela. New Brunswick, NJ: Transaction Books, 1982.

Alexander, Robert J. The Venezuelan Democratic Revolution. New Brunswick, NJ: Rutgers University Press, 1964.

Blanco, Marcelino et. al. Un Hombre Llamado Rómulo Betancourt. Caracas: Catala/Centauro/Editores, 1975.

Blanco, Penalver, P. Lopez Contreras Ante la Historia. Caracas: Tip. Garrido; 1957.

Burggraaf, Winfield J. The Venezuelan Armed Forces in Politics: 1935-1959. Colombia, MO: University of Missouri Press, 1972.

Chester, David Wayne. "The Venezuelan Junta de Gobierno of 1958: from Dictatorship to Constitutional Government." Unpublished MA thesis, University of Virginia, 1972.

Gil Yepes, Jose Antonio. The Challenge of Venezuelan Democracy. New Brunswick, NJ: Transaction Books, 1981.

Gonzalez Herrara, Luis. Rómulo en Berna. Caracas: Ediciones Centauro, 1978.

Herman, Donald. Christian Democracy in Venezuela. Chapel Hill, NC: The University of North Carolina Press, 1980.

Levine, Daniel H. Conflict and Political Change in Venezuela. Princeton: Princeton University Press, 1973.

Liscano, Juan and Carlos Gottberg. Multimagen de Rómulo. Caracas: Editora ORBECA, 1978.

Magallanes, Manuel Vicente. Los Partidos Políticos en la Evolucion Historica de Venezuela. Caracas: Monte Avila Editores, 1977.

Magallanes, Manuel Vicente. Partidos Políticos Venezolanos. Caracas: Tipografia Vargas, 1959.

Martz, John D. Acción Democrática: Evolution of a Modern Political Party in Venezuela. Princeton: Princeton University Press, 1966.

Martz, John D. and David J. Myers (eds). Venezuela: The Democratic Experience. New York: Praeger Publishers, 1977.

Njalam, Humberto et. al. El Sistema Político Venezolano. Instituto de Estudios Politicos: University Central de Venezuela, 1975.

Serxner, Stanley J. Acción Democrática of Venezuela: Its Origin and Development. Gainesville, FL: University of Florida Latin American Monographs, No. 9, September, 1959.

Suarez Figueroa, Naudy. Programas Politicos Venezolanos de la Primera Mitad del Siglo XX. Caracas: Universidad Catolica Andres Bello, 1977.

Sucre, Maria de Lourdes. La Generacion Venezolano de 1928. Caracas: Ed. Ariel 1967.

Velasquez, Ramon J. Betancourt en la Historia de Venezuela del Siglo XX. Caracas: Ed. Centauro, 1980.

171

Argentina

Canton, Dario. Argentina: la Democracia Constitucional y su Crisis. Buenos Aires: Paidos, 1972.

Fern, H. S. Argentina. New York: Frederick A. Praeger, 1969.

Giuffra, Eduardo F. Hipólito Yrigoyen en la Historia de las Instituciones Argentinas. Buenos Aires: Ed. de la Fundacion, 1969.

Goldwert, Marvin. Democracy, Militarism, and Nationalism in Argentina, 1930-1966. Austin, TX: University of Texas Press, 1972.

Gulletti, Alfredo. La Política y los Partidos. Mexico: Fondo de la Cultura Economica, 1961.

Inigo Carrera, Hector. La Experiencia Radical, 1916-1922. Buenos Aires: Ed. La Bastilla, 1980.

Landa, Jose. Hipólito Yrigoyen Visto por Uno de Sus Medicos. Buenos Aires: Macland SRL, 1958.

Luna, Felix. Yrigoyen. Buenos Aires: Editorial el Coloquio, 1975.

MacDonald, Austin F. Government of the Argentine Republic. New York: Thomas Y. Crowell Co., 1942.

del Mazo, Gabriel. Breve Historia del Radicalismo. Buenos Aires: Compañia Editora y Distribuidora de Plata, 1964.

del Mazo, Gabriel. El Pensamiento Escrito de Yrigoyen. Cordoba, Argentina: Union Civica Radical, 1976.

del Mazo, Gabriel. El Radicalismo. Buenos Aires: ed. Raigal, 1955.

del Mazo, Gabriel. Política Internacional Americana del Presidente Yrigoyen. Montevideo: Consejo Departamental de Montevideo, 1960.

del Mazo, Gabriel. Vida de un Político Argentino. Buenos Aires: Editorial Plus Ultra, 1976.

Moro, Atilio (ed). Yrigoyen: Proceso a su Gobierno. Buenos Aires: n.p., 1929.

Munson, Frederick P. and Thomas E. Weil. Area Handbook for Argentina. Washington: US GPO, 1969.

Pena, Milciades. Masas, Caudillos, y Elites: La Dependencia Argentina de Yrigoyen a Peron. Buenos Aires: Ediciones Fichas, 1971.

Potash, Robert. El Ejercito y la Politica en la Argentina: 1928-1945. Buenos Aires: Editorial Sudamerica, 1971.

Rock, David (ed). Argentina in the Twentieth Century. Pittsburgh: University of Pittsburgh Press, 1975.

Rock, David. Politics in Argentina, 1890-1930: The Rise and Fall of Radicalism. Cambridge, Cambridge University Press, 1975.

Scalabrini Ortiz, Raul. Yrigoyen y Peron. Buenos Aires: Plus Ultra, 1973.

Scobie, James R. Argentina: A City and a Nation. New York: Oxford University Press, 1964.

Silva, Francisco V. (ed). Semblanzas de Yrigoyen.

172

Buenos Aires: Talleres Graficas Argentinos L. J.
Rosso, 1938.
Sivori, Jose F. El Presidente Yrigoyen. Buenos Aires:
Talleres Graficos Buenos Aires de la UCR del
Pueblo, 1961.
Snow, Peter G. Political Forces in Argentina. New
York: Praeger Publishers, 1979.
Sommi, Luis V. Hipolito Yrigoyen: Su Vida y Su Epoca.
Buenos Aires: Editorial Monteagudo, 1947.
Yrigoyen, Hipólito. Mi Vida y Mi Doctrina. Buenos
Aires: Ed. Leviatan, 1981.

Chile

Alessandri, Arturo, et. al. El Presidente Alessandri a
Traves de Sus Discursos y Actuacion Politica.
Santiago de Chile: Biblioteca Americana, 1926.
Alessandri Palma, Arturo. Recuerdos de Gobierno.
Santiago, Chile: Editorial Nascimiento, 3 vols.,
1967.
Arañeda Bravo, Fidel. Arturo Alessandri Palma.
Santiago, Chile: Editorial Nascimiento, 1979.
Brayo Lira, Bernardino. Regimen de Gobierno y Partidos
Políticos de Chile, 1924-1973. Santiago: Ed.
Juridica de Chile, 1978.
Burnett, Ben G. Political Groups in Chile. Austin,
Texas: University of Texas Press, 1970.
Caviedos, Cesar L. The Politics of Chile: A Socio-
graphical Assessment. Boulder: Westview Press,
1979.
Donoso, Ricardo. Alessandri: Agitador y Demoledor. 2
vols. Mexico: Fondo de la Cultura Economica,
1954.
Duran Bernales Florencio. El Partido Radical. Santiago
de Chile: Ed. Nascimiento, 1958.
Figueroa, Virgilio. Diccionario Histórico y Biográfico
de Chile. Nendeln, Liechtenstein: Kraus-Thomson
Organization, 1974.
Galdames, Luis (tr. Isaac Joslin Cox). A History of
Chile. Chapel Hill: The University of North
Carolina Press, 1941.
Gil, Federico. The Political System of Chile. Boston:
Houghton-Mifflin, 1966.
Haring, Clarence. "Chilean Politics: 1900-1928,"
Hispanic American Historical Review. XI, No. 1
(February, 1931), 1-21.
Iglesias, Augusto. Alessandri: Una Etapa de la
Democracia en America. Santiago, Chile: Editorial
Andres Bello, 1960.
Moreno, Francisco Jose. Legitimacy and Stability in
Latin America: A Study of Chilean Political
Culture. New York: New York University Press,
1969.

Nunn, Fredrick M. "Military Rule in Chile: The Revolutions of September 5, 1924, and January 23, 1925," Hispanic American Historical Review. XLVII, No. 1 (February, 1967), 1-21.

Orrego, Claudio, et. al. 7 Ensayos Sobre Arturo Alessandri Palma. Santiago de Chile: Instituto Chileno de Estudios Humanisticos, 1979.

Petras, James. Politics and Social Forces in Chilean Development. Berkeley, California: University of California Press, 1969.

Pinto Lagarrigue, Fernando. Crónica Política del Siglo XX. Santiago de Chile: Editorial Orbe, 1972.

Tarr, Terence S. "Military Intervention and Civilian Reaction in Chile, 1924-1936." Unpublished PhD Dissertation, University of Florida, 1960.

Cuba

Acuña, Juan Antonio. Cuba: Revolucion Frustrada? Montevideo: n.p., 1960.

Aguilar, Luis E. Cuba 1933: Prologue to Revolution. Ithaca: Cornell University Press, 1972.

Beals, Carleton. The Crime of Cuba. Philadelphia: J. B. Lippincott, 1933.

Benjamin, Jules Robert. The United States and Cuba: Hegemony and Dependent Development, 1889-1934. Pittsburgh: University of Pittsburgh Press, 1974.

Chapman, Charles E. A History of the Cuban Republic. New York: The MacMillan Company, 1927.

Dominguez, Jorge I. Cuba: Order and Revolution. Cambridge: Harvard University Press, 1978.

Farber, Samuel. Revolution and Reaction in Cuba, 1933-1960. Middletown: Wesleyan University Press, 1966.

Fitzgibbon, Russell H. Cuba and the United States. New York: Russell and Russell, 1964.

Figerola, Joel James. Cuba 1900-1928: La República Dividida Contra Si Misma. La Habana: Editorial Arte y Literatura, 1976.

Gellman, Irwin F. Roosevelt and Batista. Albuquerque: University of New Mexico Press, 1973.

Perez, Louis A. Intervention, Revolution, and Politics in Cuba, 1913-1921. Pittsburgh: University of Pittsburgh Press, 1978.

Raby, D. L. The Cuban Pre-Revolution of 1933: An Analysis. Glasgow: University of Glasgow Occasional Papers, 1975.

Ruiz, Ramon Eduardo. Cuba: The Making of a Revolution. New York: W. W. Norton, 1970.

Smith, Robert F. Background to Revolution. New York: Alfred A. Knopf, 1966.

Strode, Hudson. The Pageant of Cuba. New York: Harrison Smith and Robert Haas, 1934.

174

Tabares de Real, Jose A. La Revolucion del 30: Sus Dos Ultimos Años. La Habana: Editorial de Ciencias Sociales, 1973.

Thomas, Hugh. Cuba: The Pursuit of Freedom. New York: Harper and Row, 1971.

El Salvador

Anderson, Thomas P. Matanza: El Salvador's Communist Revolt of 1932. Lincoln: University of Nebraska Press, 1971.

Arnson, Cynthia. El Salvador: The Revolution Confronts the United States. Washington: Institute for Policy Studies, 1982.

Baily, John et. al. El Salvador de 1840 a 1935. San Salvador: UCA/Editores, 1978.

Baron Ferrufino, Jose Rene. Comunismo y Traicion. San Salvador: Editorial Ahora, 1971.

Castaneda, Francisco. El General Menendez y Sus Victimarios. Ministerio de Education: San Salvador, 1966.

Dalton, Roque. Miguel Marmol: los Sucesos de 1932 en El Salvador. San Jose: Editorial Universitaria Centroamericana, 1972.

Didion, Joan. Salvador. New York: Simon and Schuster, 1983.

Gavida, Francisco. Historia Moderna de El Salvador. San Salvador: Ministerio de Cultura, 1958.

Gettleman, Marvin, et. al. (eds). El Salvador: Central America in the New Cold War. New York: Grove Press, 1981.

Guidos Vejar, Rafael. El Ascenso del Militarismo en El Salvador. San Salvador: UCA/Editores, 1980.

Kennedy, Paul P. The Middle Beat: A Correspondent's View of Mexico, Guatemala, and El Salvador. New York: Teacher's College Press, 1971.

Leisterschneider, Mari and Freddy Leistenschneider. Gobernantes de El Salvador. San Salvador: Imprenta Nacional, 1980.

Microfilm. "Confidential US Diplomatic Post Records: Central America, El Salvador, 1930-1945." University Publications of America, 1983.

Peña Kampy, Alberto. El General Martinez: Un Patriarcal Presidente Dictador. San Salvador: Editorial Tipografica Ramirez, 1972.

Rodriquez, Mario. Central America. Englewood Cliffs, NJ: Prentice-Hall, Inc., 1965.

Salazar Valiente, Mario. El Proceso Politico Centroamericano. San Salvador: Editorial Universitaria, 1964.

White, Alastair. El Salvador. London: Ernest Benn Limited, 1973.

Peru

Aguirre Gamin, Hernando. Liquidacion Histórica del APRA
    y del Colonialismo Neoliberal. Lima: Ed. Debate,
    1962.
Alexander, Robert J. (ed). Aprismo: The Ideas and
    Doctrines of Victor Raul Haya de la Torre. Kent,
    Ohio: Kent State University Press, 1973.
Alisky, Marvin. Peruvian Political Perspective. Tempe:
    Center for Latin American Studies, Arizona State
    University Press, 1972.
Bourricaud, Francois. Power and Society in Contemporary
    Peru. New York: Praeger Publishers, 1967 (tr.
    Paul Stevenson).
Chirinos Soto, Enrique. Historia de la Republica: Peru,
    1920-1978. Lima: Editorial Andina, 1977.
Cossio del Pomar, F. Haya de la Torre El Indoamericano.
    Mexico City: Editorial America, 1939.
Cossio del Pomar, Felipe. Victor Raul: Biografia de
    Haya de la Torre. Mexico City: Editorial Cultura,
    1961.
de la Guarda, Manuel Cesar. Aprismo: Cancer Social.
    Santiago, Chile: Editorial Indo-Americana, 1938.
Guardia Mayorga, C. A. Construyendo El Aprismo.
    Arequipa, Peru: Tipografia Acosta, 1945.
Haya de la Torre, Victor Raul. Obras Completas (Vol's
    1-7). Lima: Libreria-Editorial Juan Mejia Baca,
    1976.
Hilliker, Grant. The Politics of Reform in Peru: The
    Aprista and Other Mass Parties of Latin America.
    Baltimore: John Hopkins Press, 1971.
Kantor, Harry. The Ideology and Program of the Peruvian
    Aprista Movement. New York: Octagon Books, 1966.
Murillo Garaycochea, Percy. Historia del APRA: 1919-
    1945. Lima: Imprenta Editora Atlantida, S. A.,
    1977.
Owens, R. J. Peru. London: Oxford University Press,
    1963.
Palmer, David S. Peru: The Authoritarian Tradition.
    New York, Praeger, 1980.
Payne, James L. Labor and Politics in Peru. New Haven:
    Yale University Press, 1965.
Pike, Frederick. A Modern History of Peru. London and
    New York, 1967.
Sanchez, Luis Alberto. Biografía del APRA. Lima:
    Mosca Azul Editores, 1978.
Sanchez, Luis Alberto. Haya de la Torre o El Político:
    Cronica de Una Vida sin Tregua. Santiago, Chile:
    Ediciones Ercilla, 1934.
Sanchez, Luis Alberto. Una Larga Guerra Civil. Lima:
    Mosca Azul Editores, 1979.
Tavara, Santiago. Historia de los Partidos. Lima:
    Huascaran, 1951.
Werlick, David W. Peru: A Short History. Carbondale,
    Illinois: Southern Illinois University Press, 1978.

Index

Acción Democrática (Venezuela) 12, 16-17, 73-76, 163. See also Rómulo Betancourt.
actor dispensability, 36, 107, 149-151
Alem, Leandro 83-85
Alessandri, Arturo 2, 6, 20, 94-102, 151. See also political personality; Unión Cívica Radical (Argentina).
Alianza Popular Revolucionaria (APRA) 10, 117-133. See also Victor Raul Haya de la Torre.
Auténticos (Cuba) 109-111. See also Ramón Grau San Martín.

Balaguer Joaquin 58-60
Batista, Fulgencio 106
Belaunde y Terry, Fernando 129-130
Betancourt, Rómulo 2, 9, 29, 63-76, 162-164. See also political personality; Acción Democrática
Burns, James McGregor 11, 23-24, 147, 151, 153

Caffery, Jefferson 107, 139, 140.
Calles, Plutarco Elias 2, 8, 10, 20, 29, 32, 34-42, 162-163. See also political person-

ality; Partido Revolucionario Institucional.
Castro, Fidel 104-111
caudillos. See dictators.
continuismo 34, 76
COPEI (Venezuela) 63, 71-72

democracy in Latin America 8-10
dictators 1-2, 6-7, 11, 17, 33, 35, 39-40, 43, 65, 89
  in Venezuela 64-68
  in Dominican Republic 50-52
  in Cuba 105

Generation of '28 8, 63, 67
Gomez Juan Vicente 64-66
Grau San Martín Ramón 32-33, 106-115. See also Political personality; Auténticos.
Greenstein, Fred 20, 149

Haya de la Torre, Victor Raul 2, 8, 32, 117-133. See also Political personality Alianza Popular Revolucionaria Americana.
Hernandez Martinez, Maximiliano 137-145. See also political personality.
Heureaux, Ulises 50-51

Institutionalization 1, 29,

176